Paradise on Earth

Exploring a Christian response to suffering

Luke Bell

*When you get to this point, that tribulation is sweet to you
and you savour it for Christ, then consider it is well with
you, because you have found paradise on earth.*

Thomas à Kempis

Kevin
Mayhew

First published in 1993 by
KEVIN MAYHEW LTD
Rattlesden
Bury St Edmunds
Suffolk IP30 0SZ

ISBN   0 86209 481 X

© Cover: *Sunrise* Photograph used with permission.
Quidenham Cards, Carmelite Monastery,
Quidenham NR16 2PH

Cover design by Graham Johnstone
Printed and bound in Great Britain.

For St Thérèse of the Child Jesus and of the Holy Face

ACKNOWLEDGEMENTS: This book grew out of a correspondence with Dr Philip Holt, and owes its birth to his encouragement. His observations account for a large part of any lack of muddle and obscurity in it. My thanks are due to Stephen Cviić, my brothers Jonathan and Julian Bell and several of my monastic brethren for reading a draft and helping by suggesting corrections and giving encouragement. My editor, Michael Forster, has given invaluable help in preparing the text for publication.

The author and publishers wish to thank the following:

The Samuel Beckett Estate and The Calder Educational Trust, London, for permission to quote from the following works by Samuel Beckett:

Proust & Three Dialogues with Georges Duthuit, John Calder (Publishers) Ltd., London. Copyright © Samuel Beckett 1931, 1949, 1965, 1970, 1987.

Ill Seen Ill Said, translated by Samuel Beckett, John Calder (Publishers) Ltd., London. Copyright © Samuel Beckett 1981, 1982.

The Samuel Beckett Trilogy, John Calder (Publishers) Ltd., London. Copyright © Samuel Beckett 1959, 1976; comprising *Molloy*, translated by Samuel Beckett in association with Patrick Bowles, copyright © Samuel Beckett 1950, 1955, 1959, 1976; *Malone Dies*, translated by Samuel Beckett, copyright © Samuel Beckett 1956, 1959, 1976; *The Unnamable*, copyright © Samuel Beckett 1958, 1959, 1976.

A. P. Watt Ltd on behalf of The Grail, England, for permission to quote from *The Psalms: A New Translation* published by HarperCollins Publishers.

Faber and Faber Ltd (Publishers) for permission to quote from *Four Quartets* by T. S. Eliot.

William Heinemann for permission to quote from *The Brothers Karamazov*, Book 2, Chapter 4, by Dostoevsky.

CONTENTS

FOREWORD

The scope of this book

The title of this book is taken from this sentence in the last chapter of the second book of Thomas à Kempis' *The Imitation of Christ*: 'When you get to this point, that tribulation is sweet to you and you savour it for Christ, then consider it is well with you, because you have found paradise on earth.' Its aim is to see how it can be possible for 'tribulation' to be 'sweet'. Taking à Kempis' saying as its starting point, it seeks to understand how suffering can be a means of joyful spiritual growth. It should be emphasised that it is concerned with unavoidable suffering that cannot be relieved, or suffering that is freely undertaken as the lesser evil to someone else being hurt. It is in no way intended as a complete answer to the problem of pain, and should not be used as such. There are vast and vital areas of concern to do with fighting injustice and relief of suffering, upon which it does not touch. This limitation of the book's scope is in no way intended to detract from the importance of these concerns. It is very important to work to lessen suffering. Although the book's focus is on individual suffering, it does not thereby mean to imply that there is any value in dwelling on one's own sufferings, still less of course that there is any justification for insensitivity to others' suffering. Suffering on one's own is on the whole more difficult than when it is the common lot, since in the latter case it can become a means of people coming closer to each other; so if we can understand how this can be a means of joyful spiritual growth, we have understood the more difficult case. It is of course possible – and indeed desirable – for joyful spiritual growth to take place in a community as a whole, but even a single seed can bear much fruit and if we can understand the spiritual alchemy that transforms the dross of suffering into the gold of supernatural joy for one person then we will also have a grasp of the principles according to which whole societies can be transformed in this way. We will know how God's peace and joy enter this world although they are not of this world.

CHAPTER ONE

THE CHALLENGE

*How can spiritual masters talk of finding
joy in suffering*

'When you get to this point, that tribulation is sweet to you and you savour it for Christ, then consider it is well with you, because you have found paradise on earth', wrote à Kempis in *The Imitation of Christ*.[1] Similar statements are to be found in other spiritual writing. For example, Meister Eckhart writes in *The Book of Divine Comfort*: 'If we were in a right state, our suffering would be no suffering, but a joy and comfort'.[2] Louis de Blois, a sixteenth-century abbot, writes in his *Book of Spiritual Instruction* that suffering tribulation may be called 'the ring, adorned with a glittering stone of priceless worth, by which God espouses the soul to himself'.[3] St Thérèse of Lisieux seems deliberately to echo à Kempis in her words: 'I have come to the point of not being able to suffer any more, because all suffering is sweet to me'.[4] This declaration of à Kempis, 'When you get to this point, that tribulation is sweet to you and you savour it for Christ, then consider it is well with you, because you have found paradise on earth', echoed by many spiritual writers and saints, presents a challenge: how can it be true? How can we imagine a state where tribulation, which we are accustomed to think of as making us, almost by definition, miserable and depressed, is sweet to us? What sort of attitude, mind or soul does a person in this state have? How can we imagine the customary negative reaction to tribulation – anxiety and depression – transformed to *this* extent? Can 'this point' be reached? If so, what is the road to it?

This book attempts to face this challenge. It is written in the conviction that 'paradise on earth' is a real human possibility. It is a bold claim, but it is not a claim that the writer himself has reached 'this point'. The claim is rather that the lives and words of saints provide clear evidence that people have reached it. This book is an exposition of their teaching: it lays claim to no new ideas or discoveries. Two saints in particular are a source of inspiration for it. The first, St John of the Cross, will remain in the background, but the thinking and the structure of the book is much indebted to him. The second, his disciple, St Thérèse of Lisieux, will be invited to show us more directly what reaching 'this point' means. As for the writer, he appeals to the saying of St John Climacus, the desert father, who counselled: 'Anyone in the grip of previous bad habits and yet still able to give teaching, although only by their words, should do so', observing that 'shamed by their own words, they may finally begin to practise what they preach'![5] If in years to come, any reader should seek me out and find me narrowed and embittered by suffering, that does not invalidate the experience of saints for whom suffering has been a means of growth. My words are no more than a homage to such people, and to all who suffer.

I am sensitive to the fact that to write on a subject related to suffering is to risk adding insult to the injuries of those who do suffer. I write in the spirit of reverence for suffering shown by the elder Zossima, in Dostoevsky's novel, *The Brothers Kara-mazov*, who prostrates himself before one of the brothers, Dmitri, because he knows Dmitri is to suffer greatly.[6] I write as a pupil learning from a master, who is anyone at all who suffers. I know that St Thérèse spoke the truth when she said, within a week of her death, 'It's very easy to write fine things about suffering, but to write is nothing, nothing! One has to be in it to know!'[7] To anyone who is mentally crushed I say 'you know more than I do'.

In a sense, however, this book is not focused on suffering. It is focused rather on an attitude that enables its joyful acceptance. The joy in no way comes from the suffering itself: this attitude is as far as it could be from masochism. The book attempts to understand the attitude, what is conducive to it and what it consists of. The understanding sought is partly analytical and partly imaginative. It is analytical to the extent that it separates the various aspects of it, and stages on the way to it. It is imaginative in the way that it attempts to answer the natural response to à Kempis' statement: 'Well, I can imagine someone being brave about tribulation, or putting up with it, but I can't imagine in what possible sense someone so afflicted could be enjoying paradise on earth'. So much of our failure is a failure to imagine what could be possible for us, rather than a failure in abstract thinking. It is difficult for us to adopt an attitude we cannot imagine. It is important to add to a rational grasp of its possibility an imaginative understanding of how this attitude could really be approached. This is the reason for giving extensive illustrations from literature and discussing them. It is hoped these will help the heart as well as the mind to understand, and that they will show that the questions dealt with concern not only the consciously religious but all who ponder human experience. Poetry predominates, since in dealing with something as delicate of definition as attitude, only poetry's capacity to capture nuance is really adequate. It is so easy for an attitude to disguise itself, passing muster under what might reasonably be considered an adequate legal definition of its opposite. Uriah Heep, for example, asserts himself by the rules of humility. Also, this book is an invitation to share a quest, and as such needs to appeal to the imagination. Travel brochures without pictures can't be expected to sell many holidays – not even when they speak of paradise!

The remainder of this chapter lists, as it were, the contents of the brochure. The next chapter examines a couple of examples of tribulation borne in a way that echoes à Kempis' saying. By looking at these we can hope to get some impression of what the attitude is that makes of suffering a means of joyful growth, before we go on to consider that attitude's foundational principles. The chapter also discusses various hints offered by common experience of the possibility of positive attitudes emerging in one who suffers: intimations that tribulation could be the grit that produces the pearl. If we can see the seeds of this way of taking suffering in ordinary lives, we shall be better placed to understand the examples of the saints as a development of a potential that we ourselves have.

These examples and hints suggest that there is dignity and indeed great possibility for good in how a person reacts to what they are unable to control. Nobility of character and goodness are located here to a greater extent than is perhaps generally realised at the present time. Given the technological efficiency of modern society, the tendency is to think of a person's dignity in terms of how they can control (if not manipulate) their environment. This alone, however, cannot give a person ultimate dignity, since all such activity is in the end defeated by death. There are important values relating to how we react to the bad things we cannot change, as well as important values relating to how we accept the challenge to change what is bad where this is possible. These values are to do with nobility of character and goodness.

This suggests that the journey along the road to 'this point' – where tribulation becomes sweet in the manner described by à Kempis – begins with some kind of conversion. The third and fourth chapters deal with this. It is a conversion to an inner life that is envisaged, the cultivation of an attitude of freedom and detachment as opposed to a possessive and grasping one. The value and difficulty of this is discussed in these chapters. Its value is transcendent, but its difficulty is that lesser goals present themselves more readily, to claim an absolute attention of which they are not worthy. It is argued that suffering, rightly used, can be a means by which one can be steered from the lesser to the transcendent. An attitude of unpossessive freedom (or openness to the transcendent) is not normally acquired overnight, so the question arises of how a person can grow in it. The next three pairs of chapters deal respectively with the theological virtues of faith, hope and love that foster this growth, this conversion. These virtues strengthen the inner life that frees a person from being absolutely bound by what is temporary, and roots them in the true and ever-creative absolute that is God himself. They are examined in these chapters with a view to understanding how unavoidable suffering can become a means towards their growth and therefore a person's movement from bondage to freedom. Each of these virtues brings with it the other two and the discussion is not divided in such a way that each pair of chapters is devoted exclusively to the virtue concerned.

The writing is of a reflective nature that develops implications and suggestions. It may however help establish a sense of its direction and purpose if it is borne in mind that it is basically concerned with the growth of the soul in these virtues. If this growth is a primary goal and its fulfilment the deepest joy, and if we can see how 'tribulation' can be a means to it, then we shall be able to see how à Kempis is able to speak of its being called 'sweet'.

Growth in faith, hope and love is growth in the life of God. The more a person grows in this, the more they see everything from this point of view, the way God sees it. This is the only point of view from which everything, including all tribulations, makes sense. So it is to be expected that to the extent that someone comes to see everything from here, he will be able to see it all as part of a greater harmony. The pains will no longer be seen in isolation and darkness, but as belonging to a greater pattern. There will be an intuitive sense of the whole tapestry, not just the knots that the individual behind it is tying. The drumbeat of the solitary percussionist will be exchanged for the sound of the whole orchestra. The single syllable of the poem will take its place in the whole. Only in God is this sense of unity and therefore meaning possible. We shall be concerned with the spiritual growth that brings the unfolding of this meaning.

The eleventh chapter turns from the analysis of how this spiritual growth and unity in life (or integrity) can be achieved, to look at an exemplar of it: St Thérèse of Lisieux. Lest it be thought that it is an abstraction existing 'only in a world of speculation'[8] the focus is on a particular tribulation and how it was borne, picking up again the discussion of tribulation in the second chapter. It is presented in the belief that, as is said of Cordelia in *King Lear*,

> Sorrow would be a rarity most beloved,
> If all could so become it.[9]

The present chapter has offered a summary of the book: the final chapter presents the summing-up of mankind, Jesus Christ, who alone can provide the grace that enables the attitude sought. It considers how his life is the epitome of this attitude. It looks at its presentation in ritual and asks the question: 'What does the world look like to someone who has found paradise on earth?'

CHAPTER TWO

TRIBULATION

Some examples of troubles
constructively borne

À Kempis talks of 'tribulation' being 'sweet' and being savoured 'for Christ'. If we are to understand how this can be so, we need first of all to see some examples of this happening and see them as much as possible from inside the mind of the person concerned. The aim of this chapter is to provide them. One example will draw on the imagination of a poet to try to understand how it might be possible to 'savour' something terrible 'for Christ', and the other on the insight of a saint into her own life to see how something annoying can be undergone in a positive way. We shall also consider 'tribulation' in every-day experience and look for clues that this can give us as to the sense in which it might be found 'sweet'.

'Tribulation' has a wide scope of meaning. The obvious sense of the word is as referring to some major personal disaster, suffering or bereavement. Tribulation in this sense is the subject of Gerard Manley Hopkins' *The Wreck of the Deutschland*. The poem in fact presents an example of someone who finds tribulation sweet and savours it for the sake of Christ. It describes the death by drowning of five Franciscan nuns. According to *The Times* of December 11th 1875, they

> were drowned together, the chief sister, a gaunt woman 6ft. high, calling out loudly and often 'O Christ, come quickly!' till the end came.[1]

Hopkins describes her so calling and comments:

> The cross to her she calls Christ to her, christens her
> wild-worst Best.[2]

The ambiguity of the line is an illuminating comment on à Kempis' sentence. 'The cross to her she calls Christ to her' can simply mean 'her cross having come to her, she calls upon Christ'; it can also mean 'she calls the cross that has come to her, Christ'. The first leads to the second. Having invoked Christ, her suffering becomes an experience of his presence: the touch of God, present in all things except sin, is felt. The second half of the line is similarly ambiguous. She 'christens her wild-worst Best' can simply mean she makes the best of this terrible thing that is happening to her. She calls it 'best'.

This implies she sees it as God's will for her and therefore, in the light of eternity, the best thing for her. The capital letter that begins 'Best' implies more, however, as in the phrase in Shakespeare's *The Winter's Tale*: 'My name/Be yok'd with his that did betray the Best'.[3] The Best, the first-born from the dead, is Christ himself, the personification of good. When she 'christens her wild-worst Best' she makes her experience of the 'wild-worst' an experience of Christ, christens it, by living it in and through him. Because he is in it, it is transformed. The second half of the line, then, echoes the first.

This interpretation is borne out by the subsequent stanzas. The next three dismiss the idea that she was thinking of her reward in Heaven or that she was meditating upon Christ's own suffering, and the stanza presents, as though it were bursting into the poet's mind, the presence of Christ to her. Upon this there is this comment:

> Ah! there was a heart aright!
> There was single eye!
> Read the unshapeable shock night
> And knew the who and the why;
> Wording it how but by him that present and past,
> Heaven and earth are word of, worded by? −[4]

The 'single eye' alludes to St Luke chapter 11 verse 34: 'When your eye is sound, your whole body is full of light'. The first two lines imply that she saw and felt rightly, the second two that she understood her tribulation. In 'the unshapeable shock night', an apparently meaningless blow, she saw a personal meaning: 'the who and the why'. She savours it for

Christ and he becomes its savour for her. She words it – sees meaning in it – through the Word through whom all things were made. He is present and past: eternal source both of the creation and of meaning to the darkest experiences within it.

This heroism of the nun is an example of an extreme situation which evokes a response, and there is a sense in which this kind of tribulation is easier to bear precisely because it is so demanding. Hopkins observes, in his other poem about a shipwreck:

> It is even seen, time's something server,
> In mankind's medley a duty-swerver,
>   At downright 'No or Yes?'
> Doffs all, drives full for righteousness.[5]

It is a common occurrence that an extreme situation will be an occasion to which someone will rise. Those bereaved will sometimes devote themselves to a good cause that aims to help those that suffer in a similar way to the one who died. They may become very emotionally open to others, very grateful for anything that is done for them. There is, however, tribulation of another kind where these responses tend not to be evoked. Our search for an explanation of à Kempis' saying needs to include this as well. It is the tribulation of constant minor irritation. Two examples of this are given by St Thérèse in her autobiography in her discussion of her struggle to practice fraternal charity. First she describes a sister in front of whom she was placed during the evening prayer:

> As soon as this sister had arrived, she started to make a strange little sound which resembled that one would make rubbing two shells one against another. It was only me who noticed it, because I have an extremely sharp ear (a bit too much sometimes). To tell you, my Mother, how much this little noise tired me would be impossible: I very much wanted to turn my head and look at the guilty party who, of course, didn't notice her mannerism, it was the only way to enlighten her; but at the bottom

of my heart I felt that it would be better to suffer it for the love of God and so as not to distress the sister. So I stayed calm, I tried to unite myself with the good God, to forget the little noise. . . all was useless, I felt the sweat drenching me and I was obliged simply to offer a prayer of suffering, but while suffering I tried not to do so with irritation, but with joy and peace, at least in the intimacy of my soul. So I tried to love this little noise that was so unpleasant; instead of trying not to hear it (which was impossible) I turned my attention to listening to it well, as if it had been a ravishing concert and all my prayer (which wasn't that of *quiet*) was spent in offering this concert to Jesus.

Another time, I was at the washing in front of a sister who splashed dirty water on my face each time she lifted up the handkerchieves on the bench; my first impulse was to recoil wiping my face to show the sister who was sprinkling me that she would be doing me a favour by behaving calmly, but immediately I thought that it was really stupid to refuse the treasures that were given to me so generously and I checked myself from letting my struggle appear. I made every effort to desire to receive a lot of dirty water, so in the end I had really acquired a taste for this new kind of aspersion and I promised myself to come back another time to this happy place where I had received so many treasures.[6]

St Thérèse's account of her loving acceptance of these irritations really contains the seed of the explanation of our quotation from à Kempis. On a small scale here are the attitudes that would enable her to find joy and peace even in the greatest suffering. We shall be examining what constitutes them more fully in later chapters, especially Chapter Nine. The point here is that they are relevant to both minor and major tribulation: in a way her response here is more impressive than that of the nun in the storm, because there is no big challenge to stimulate it and because it has to be maintained over a long period of time.

Both of these nuns show that they have reached the point described by à Kempis. This may however seem remote and rather unimaginable in the face of common experience, which sometimes seems to suggest that a person is doomed to a constant level of anxiety and discontent. If one thing is not a source of worry, another will become so. There is a kind of free-floating anxiety always wanting something to latch onto. There is a similar irritation which will be transferred from one person to another when the former is no longer available. These states seem to be imprisoning: changes of pasture don't remove them. It is as though the exact causes of tribulation are irrelevant: it is simply part of life. One of Samuel Beckett's characters seems to imply as much when he complains of the mania for diagnosis:

> People are never content to suffer, but they must have heat and cold, rain and its contrary which is fine weather, and with that love, friendship, black skin and sexual and peptic deficiency for example, in short the furies and frenzies happily too numerous to be numbered of the body including the skull and its annexes, whatever that means, such as the club-foot, in order that they may know very precisely what it is that dares prevent their happiness being unalloyed.[7]

This malaise, this discontent looking for something to blame, can stand as a sort of epitome of tribulation. It certainly suggests that the basic difficulty is attitudinal. One can see something of the sort in the way that what is an amusing or endearing foible to an affectionately disposed person may be an irritating fault to the more censoriously inclined. A different attitude makes for a different experience.

It is not, however, proposed that tribulation is all in the mind. That there are real causes of pain, devastatingly immediate and relentlessly trivial, is clear. In discussing how we are to journey to 'this point' we need to consider all these kinds of tribulation. Both externally imposed pain and apparently ingrained habits of mind that seem themselves to cause pain will be relevant. In both these cases a difference in attitude can be transforming.

The attitudes of these nuns may seem remote and unimaginable in the face of common experience, as though they were elect beings, apart from the rest of us. However, there are some clues provided by everyday experience as to how tribulation can have a positive aspect. They can give us some kind of indication of the seeds in human nature that are there to be grown into mustard trees that will give others shelter in times of tribulation: just as a seed of faith, according to Jesus, can grow into a great tree, so an attitude that is positive can aspire to one that is heroic. We can also look at them as natural analogies to the supernatural. Various common human experiences suggest the possible savour of suffering. Human love, for example, does not shrink from pain. A knight in love with his lady will undertake exploits in her honour and find joy, not in the danger or the wounds that come in these exploits, but in the fact that he is proving his love for her. The joy in that love means more to him than safety or comfort. On a less heroic scale, there is the experience in which one sign of a growing affection for someone is that one actually likes being contradicted by that person. It may have something to do with welcoming their impingement on one's life, a sense of the presence of the other. It is a moment of not entirely explicable tenderness. Then there is the truth in the conventional reply to thanks for trouble undertaken: 'It's a pleasure'. If we have a delight in being of service to a particular person, then 'the labour we delight in physics pain'.[8] All of this implies that there is something in the human spirit that can give meaning, even joyfully, to suffering.

Patterns of behaviour suggest this. People undertake considerable trouble for the sake of climbing mountains, exploring pot-holes, crossing deserts and so on – and not all of them would be satisfied to go by railway. People are (sometimes) grateful for the strictness of a childhood upbringing. They recognize that punishment has kept them from their worst self and trained them in ways that make life easier for them. Then there is the whole tradition of ascetic life: people undertake to bind themselves by rule to live in religious communities, they fast or even inflict physical pain on themselves. None of this is quite suffering, however, because all of it is chosen. But in a paradoxical way that very fact points to how it is possible for suffering to have a special value. When somebody undertakes a journey through difficult terrain, they like to feel the definite presence of nature in the abrasiveness of it (like oneself being contradicted). Suffering, because not asked for, is a stronger demonstration of the presence of the other, a relief from the wearying presence of the all-appropriating ego. Suffering is when one would opt, in the deluding imagination, for any trial but this one. It is otherness tearing at the self.

It is only the false self that it attacks: the pretensions to control a destiny that cannot be controlled, only co-operated with; the false security of grain in barns instead of treasure in heaven;[9] the undue sense of one's importance. In fact a truly good person cannot be hurt in any absolute or lasting way. Their good is to do the will of God: they have that good simply by wanting it and it can never be taken away from them. That person's soul is immortal and it can grow in their tribulations. This suggests the path to the point where 'tribulation is sweet'. It is the path towards unselfishness, towards being good. The chapters that follow attempt its topography, with the particular aim in view of trying to understand how, as it is followed, tribulation may come to seem sweet. Our mapping out in words, however, will not always be advancing from one stage to another: necessarily, it will go over ground more than once to bring out different aspects. An attitude that expresses itself in the action of a single moment may need many moments to be understood.

The beginning of any path towards unselfishness is conversion: a move from a hard and proud imposition of self on the world to the gentle and peaceful inner life of the spirit. The next two chapters consider this beginning.

CHAPTER THREE

THE TWO TREES

Blessed and cursed attitudes to life and its troubles

There are two possible attitudes to life. One is God-centred and brings joy and peace and the other is self-centred and 'builds a Hell in Heaven's despite'.[1] This chapter examines these attitudes with a view to gaining an imaginative under-standing of them. The greater our understanding of them, the more we shall value an ongoing conversion from the latter to the former. If we value conversion to God highly, as an exchanging of a cursed attitude for a blessed one, we will be able to understand the idea that 'tribulation' can be 'sweet' if it can become a means towards that conversion. So it is worth considering the two attitudes in some depth.

There is a very striking saying of St Catherine of Genoa to the effect that all sorrows, annoyances and afflictions are the result of spiritual or temporal ownership.[2] This comes down to saying that they come from wanting something, whether spiritual or temporal, for the self. There is a clue to under-standing it in St Thérèse's autobiography, where she says: 'Deprived of all consolation I was nonetheless the happiest of creatures, since all my desires were satisfied'.[3] She was happy because she didn't desire anything for herself, only God's will and this was being accomplished. Another comment in the autobiography illuminates the attitude: 'Joy is not found in the objects that surround us, it is found in the deepest intimacy of the soul. One can just as well possess it in a prison as in a palace. The proof is that I am happier in the Carmel, even in the midst of interior and exterior trials than in the world surrounded by the comforts of life and *above all* in the sweetness of the paternal home. . .'[4] These comments and that of St Catherine point to finding enjoyment within, in God, rather than in possessing anything. If one has an inner enjoyment of God through love, the leaving of outward enjoyment doesn't matter greatly. One can be told what Adam is told by the Archangel Michael in Milton's *Paradise Lost*:

> then thou wilt not be loath
> To leave this Paradise, but shalt possess
> A paradise within thee, happier far.[5]

This paradise consists of the enjoyment of God through love. From this enjoyment follows the enjoyment of all creation, in which God is immanent. This is a higher enjoyment than we have in view for ourselves – before we reach the point à Kempis describes. We tend to have noticed that some particular thing gives us pleasure and to fasten on it, make it our possession. God wants us to enjoy everything in him. That is, we are made to see everything as he sees it, sharing his enjoyment of it and participating in his generosity towards it. Above all this is the generosity to let it be: he lets the sun shine and the rain fall on the just and the unjust alike;[6] he does not impose any narrowness of possession on things – he enables being to be.

The tendency of fallen man is not like this: he says, 'You can use that idea in your writing if you acknowledge your debt to me,' or, 'You are welcome to my hospitality if you are nice to me,' or, 'You can be my friend if you don't notice the wrong I do'. The perverting stamp of possession is perhaps at its most noticeably sad in human relations. 'Which of you shall we say doth love us most?'[7] asks Shakespeare's King Lear of his three daughters – he wants to control their loving response himself. But possessing the other makes a response in free (and therefore genuine) love impossible. This is not a proper enjoyment because it doesn't let the other be. Once restrictions are placed on the other – see these people if you like, but not those: you are mine – they cannot fully be, fully enjoy. The possessive tendency can extend to everything. Obviously the miser can be warped and narrowed, made cold and unsympathetic, by his attachment to money, but the scholar too can be vicious in his attacks on those who venture into that area of knowledge over which he has decided that he has authority. Possessiveness can affect the spiritual life: people can be very pleased with their own (supposed) virtue and set themselves up as correctors of others. They can cling possessively to their spiritual pleasures.

There is a story in the *Arabian Nights* about a princess who does battle with a genius. To escape he transforms himself from one creature to another as each of them is cornered by her. Finally he hides in a pomegranate seed. The princess overlooks him and, although she does finally defeat him, it is her death. In the same way possessiveness can be driven from one area of life to another and so on until it lurks, unnoticed and fatal, small and dangerous. It can affect not only our relation to things and people, but even our relation to our own experience. William Blake saw how this attitude could destroy enjoyment:

> He who binds to himself a joy
> Does the winged life destroy;
> But he who kisses the joy as it flies
> Lives in eternity's sunrise.[8]

Binding a joy to oneself is treating it possessively: trying to make it last, perhaps, longer than its time, or concentrating on the pleasure something or someone gives rather than on the thing or person. It clings to the things of time rather than being open to what God wants to give. The poem is called 'Eternity'. The detached attitude it recommends is enjoying in God, responding to the promise above promises: 'Blessed are the poor in spirit, for theirs is the kingdom of heaven'.[9] And if this is sought, all else follows: because the kingdom is a knowing of the Creator, all creation is to be enjoyed by the blessed from the single point from which it can be fully enjoyed, its source.

There are then two possible attitudes not only to things and people, but also to our very experience: poverty of spirit, which 'kisses the joy as it flies' in the light of the dawn of eternal life, and egoistic, possessive, graspingness. The first is carefree, the second is anxious and bitter. There is a kind of architectural expression of the two attitudes in the church of Santa Croce in Florence. The church itself, in romanesque style, expresses spiritual values, inviting the mind to ascend.

In it, however, are the tombs of renaissance notables which try to stamp the asserted importance of the dead upon the scene: heavy, large and unlovely, they affront the other-worldly beauty of their surroundings. These two attitudes correspond to the options presented by Moses in the book of Deuteronomy: 'I call heaven and earth to witness against you this day, that I set before you life and death, blessing and curse . . .'[10] The curse is the incomplete enjoyment, doomed to failure, that comes when the heart is drawn away to worship other gods and serve them. These are fastened upon as an absolute source of joy, when what they offer is passing and relative. Only to the absolute source of joy, the true God, can we bind ourselves without damage.

The two attitudes are given a masterly portrayal in W.B. Yeats' poem *The Two Trees*.[11] The former calls us:

> Beloved, gaze in thine own heart,
> The holy tree is growing there;
> From joy the holy branches start,
> And all the trembling flowers they bear.
> The changing colours of its fruit
> Have dowered the stars with merry light;
> The surety of its hidden root
> Has planted quiet in the night;
> The shaking of its leafy head
> Has given the waves their melody,
> And made my lips and music wed,
> Murmuring a wizard song for thee.
> There the Loves a circle go,
> The flaming circle of our days,
> Gyring, spiring to and fro
> In those great ignorant leafy ways;
> Remembering all that shaken hair
> And how the wingèd sandals dart,
> Thine eyes grow full of tender care:
> Beloved, gaze in thine own heart.

We are called to an inward joy: joy in our own heart, which comes from looking to God and knowing ourselves beloved by him. It is the opposite of the assertive extroversion that seeks an unstable delight in the possession of this or that. 'Beloved' at the beginning and the end of this part of the poem can be read as a name: it can also be a state. Beloved by God, one can look into one's own heart and see the holy tree, the cross (his and ours), and joyfully accept its blessings. This joy is the source of true creativity, 'all the trembling flowers'. It is the source of light and peace. This is not the peace that comes from knowing and understanding everything. In the obscurity of the night, quiet comes from a hidden root. It is accepted, not created. It comes from the depth of our heart where the Creator himself dwells. It leaves to him the final understanding and judgement of the dark things in our lives. The hidden joy brings with it light and peace, harmony and love. 'Melody' orders 'the Loves'. Our love is not possessive, excluding or obsessive. It does not seek in the other a means of support. It 'lives in eternity's sunrise' because 'the Loves' are not clung to, but allowed to circle according to the 'wizard song' of the hidden joy. These are 'leafy ways' because they draw their sap from the source of creation and are 'ignorant' because he is hidden in mystery. The unknown mystery of the other is respected. Drawing their strength from the uncreated light, our eyes can look out 'full of tender care'.

The second part of the poem is an admonition to avoid the contrary attitude:

> Gaze no more in the bitter glass
> The demons, with their subtle guile,
> Lift up before us when they pass,
> Or only gaze a little while;
> For there a fatal image grows
> That the stormy night receives,
> Roots half hidden under snows,
> Broken boughs and blackened leaves.
> For all things turn to barrenness
> In the dim glass the demons hold,
> The glass of outer weariness,

Made when God slept in times of old.
There, through the broken branches, go
The ravens of unresting thought;
Flying, crying, to and fro,
Cruel claw and hungry throat,
Or else they stand and sniff the wind,
And shake their ragged wings; alas!
Thy tender eyes grow all unkind:
Gaze no more in the bitter glass.

This other attitude looks not inward to that which cannot pass away, but out to that which cannot satisfy the craving of the self for its validation. To gaze at the glass, offered by the minions of the devil, is to treat the world, other people and even spiritual reality as a mirror for reflecting the self. But it is 'a fatal image' that is reflected back. If other people and things are used as a means of self-assertion, they will only reflect back the wretchedness and poverty of the self, giving a misery haunted by 'the ravens of unresting thought'. The mind, not willing humbly to trust the hidden and mysterious Creator of the universe, tries cruelly to tear knowledge from his creation and is doomed not to rest. This is the opposite of the communion offered by the harmonious love of the first attitude. It is a barren love, bereft of fecundity. Looking outward and cut off from the source of its being, the heart hardens and 'tender eyes grow all unkind'. It is not a question of the eyes enjoying what they should not: rather, they do not enjoy it well enough. They cannot see it as coming from the same source as the hidden joy within, because they are cut off from this source. All they can see is the cold egoism that they project. This is what Blake calls our 'spectre',[12] the dreary and ash-making shadow that our grasping ego casts on what we see and even what we feel.

These two attitudes are life and death, blessing and curse. Looking at them gives some notion of how tribulation may be found sweet. If comfort in outward things ('creature comfort') is denied us, this may be a providential thwarting of our seeking ourselves in them, so that we turn (converted) to seek true comfort within. It can be an awakening to God, only true rock of consolation. The pain of tribulation may be like the pain of learning to do without flattery, the echo of the sterile self offered by what is without. The truth has its cost, but it sets us free – free from the 'unresting thought' of trying to keep up the pretence that the self is the measure of all. When tribulation takes away what we love, what is threatened is not what is good and just in what we love, which is in the hands of God, but the self which was able to find its reflection in it. If that leads us away from the sterility of egoism and towards inner joy, it is a blessing.

The fact that tribulation doesn't always lead to a better attitude may have something to do with what we understand the human person to be, and so what we think has value for them. The vision of the two attitudes represented by the two trees implies a certain view of what a person is. It also implies that a movement from the bad to the good attitude has a supreme value for a person.

CHAPTER FOUR

KILLING SCHEHERAZADE

Escaping false values

The supremacy of the value of the move from the bad to the good, from the deadly to the vital, of the two attitudes described in the last chapter, implies the desirability of escaping domination by lesser values. If one has found what is alone of supreme worth – the pearl of great price[1] – then clinging to lesser goods, giving to them an over-riding importance that prevents the acquisition of the supremely worthwhile, is an evil to be avoided. To prefer the relatively unimportant, the lesser good, to the vital good is to be in the grip of a false value – like a person polishing the ash-tray in his car while driving instead of keeping his eyes on the road to avoid an accident. This chapter is concerned with the importance of escape from such false values – an escape that tribulation, rightly responded to, can aid. To understand that importance, it will be necessary to see both the limited and constricted nature of a life lived by false values and also the unlimited and unbounded vitality of a life dedicated to its true goal, the life that Jesus spoke of when he said, 'I came that they may have life, and have it abundantly'.[2]

It was once put to me, as an argument in favour of euthanasia, that an old lady at the end of her life started willingly to eat yoghurt, something she had always detested. Her identity, it was claimed, had in fact ceased. This view implies a certain idea of what a person is, one that has not understood that 'the holy tree is growing' within. The person is identified with his or her desires. A network of predilections and aversions acquired in the course of someone's life is deemed to be their very self. If one takes this view, it is very difficult to let go of the attitude that looks to 'the glass of outer weariness' for a sense of personal worth. When tribulation comes it comes thwarting predilections and aversions. It is experienced as soul-destroying because the soul is fastened upon them. The soul's suffering is not sweet because its will is being thwarted. The key to tribulation becoming sweet seems to be the detaching of the will from particular predilections and aversions: not, at any rate, taking them as absolutes that define the self – making a false god of them. To those who think that, for example, the yoghurt–abhorring persona is an absolute, this is a sort of death. Indeed it is: it is the death of egoism. The point at issue is what life there is beyond this death. Before facing this question directly, it is worth enquiring what sort of life there is before this death – that is, how vital the life is that locates itself in predilections and aversions.

This issue is faced honestly and directly by Samuel Beckett. He is sometimes thought of as a pessimistic writer: perhaps, rather, he eschews false optimism. The basic limitation of life focused on the wish for this or that is well analyzed in an early work of his, *Proust,* which is a commentary on *À La Recherche du Temps Perdu*:

> The aspirations of yesterday were valid for yesterday's ego, not for today's. We are disappointed at the nullity of what we are pleased to call attainment. But what is attainment? The identification of the subject with the object of his desire. The subject has died – and perhaps many times – on the way. For subject B to be disappointed by the banality of an object chosen by subject A is as illogical as to expect one's hunger to be dissipated by the spectacle of Uncle eating his dinner.[3]

This analysis applies to the yoghurt-abhorring persona (bad tree) self – the ego rather than the soul. It does not apply to that essential self that can look beyond the things of time to the eternal. This can identify with God's will and can accept as such things at which the ego would balk – it can find tribulation sweet. Let us consider a little more the nature of this limited life of the ego.

It is life trapped by time and space. Expressing itself in terms of hopes and fears for things that pass away it is doomed to frustration: frustration, at least, of that longing for the absolute that is mankind's undying glory. As the passage quoted above would suggest, Beckett is a poet very sensitive to the pain of life trapped in time and space. He has been described as looking like an eagle trapped behind bars in a zoo, looking wistfully at the sky. It is an apt image. His work is full of scenes that illustrate and embody, by intensification, mankind's limitation in time and space. The brevity of life is caught in a resonant image in *Waiting for Godot*: 'they give birth astride of a grave, the light gleams an instant, then it's night once more'.[4] As the oeuvre progresses the plays become increasingly short: they are haunted by time lost, by memory. An old man listens to tape-recordings of his earlier self, an old woman walks up and down 'revolving it all' in her 'poor mind'.[5] The imaging of the restrictions of space is, if anything, more intense. In *Happy Days* the heroine is buried up to her waist in a mound of earth in the first act and up to her neck in the second. Characters exist in dustbins, in urns, in a glass jar; they are confined to a bed, a rocking chair and even simply to being a mouth. If they move, it is with futility or difficulty. Vladimir and Estragon in *Waiting for Godot* don't know if they have come back to the same place; Molloy, in the novel of the same name, crawls:

> Flat on my belly, using crutches like grapnels, I plunged them ahead of me into the undergrowth, and when I felt they had a hold, I pulled myself forward, with an effort of the wrists. For my wrists were still quite strong, fortunately, in spite of my decrepitude, though all swollen and racked by a kind of chronic arthritis probably. That then, briefly, is how I went about it.[6]

This gives an impression of the bleakness of life. However, it is only the life of the ego that is bleak. The trilogy, of which *Molloy* is the first book, is concerned with the search for identity. In the third book, *The Unnameable*, the fictions of the first two books are dismissed by the voice of the narrator as not being himself. It is as though nothing in time and space can give him identity. The book ends with him still trying to find words to say who he is:

> I'll go on, you must say words, as long as there are any, until they find me, until they say me, strange pain, strange

sin, you must go on, perhaps it's done already, perhaps
they have said me already, perhaps they have carried me
to the threshold of my story, before the door that opens
on my story, that would surprise me, if it opens, it will
be I, it will be the silence, where I am, I don't know, I'll
never know, in the silence you don't know, you must go
on, I can't go on, I'll go on.[7]

He exists, not in the bustle of 'outer weariness', but 'in the
silence'. Here is the true life of the soul: not in the pursuit
through time and space of its desires and aversions, but in
communion with God. This is the life that Jesus tells us is
preserved when instead of seeking to gain our life we lose it
– lose the false life of egoism.[8] This (true) life cannot be
pinned down, cannot be named, because God is infinite. 'In
the silence you don't know': the narrator is never going to be
able to grasp his identity, his very being, the way he wants his
ego to grasp and possess things. His name can only be given
to him by God, as promised in the book of Revelation: 'To
him who conquers I will give some of the hidden manna, and
I will give him a white stone, with a new name written on the
stone which no one knows except him who receives it'.[9] The
hidden manna is the divine life of the soul and the stone is
given from, in Shelley's phrase, 'the white radiance of
Eternity'.[10] There, and not in the fulfilment of the aspirations
of yesterday's ego – the time-bound self – is his true life.

Beckett shows an awareness of that life as well as present-
ing a searchingly honest account of the limitations of existence without it. Here, in a later work, *Ill Seen Ill Said*, are an
old woman's last words:

Then in that perfect dark foreknell darling sound pip for
end begun. First last moment. Grant only enough remain
to devour all. Moment by glutton moment. Sky earth the
whole kit and boodle. Not another crumb of carrion left.
Lick chops and basta. No. One moment more. One last.
Grace to breathe that void. Know happiness.[11]

The wish to 'devour all' seems to imply a yearning for some

kind of unitive experience, or perhaps a hope of transcending creation. 'Not another crumb of carrion left' suggests the (carrion) comfort that creation offers: 'lick chops and basta' – it is to be finished with. Yet there is something beyond it – another moment. In this the woman wants 'grace to breathe that void': communion with the divine which transcends anything that occupies space and which is the source of happiness.

This moment is the dawn of the life of the soul, an intimation of eternity. It comes at the moment of death. Yet if we are to live this life fully before we die, the ego-life has in some sense to die. This is what Jesus means when he says 'If anyone comes to me and does not hate ... even his own life, he cannot be my disciple'.[12] The death of ego-life is the price of enjoying eternal life – the life of heaven, paradise – on earth. This is so, however large the range of ego-life: even if it includes the whole world, it does not profit a man to lose his soul for it.[13] Yet the ego is very tenacious of life. It is like Scheherazade, the heroine of the *Arabian Nights*. She is condemned to death, but is a consummate story teller. Each night she finishes her narration at the point where the listening monarch cannot bear to put an end to her because he wouldn't know how the story went. So it is with the things of this world by which the ego defines itself: they are only a story, insofar as they are bound by time to end, and yet they exercise a fascination that is always shifting. We learn, as it were, how one story finishes, but we want to know how the next ends. The first ending – this is a trick of narrative – seemed all important; that sense of importance, once indulged, is switched to the forthcoming ending. So it is with the desire of this and that in the world. Only in God is there an end which won't turn out not to have been the real thing.

The other things – by which the ego would assert and define itself – will not offer security. Living among them, mankind's condition is one of restlessness:

When God at first made man,
Having a glass of blessings standing by;

Let us (said he) pour on him all we can:
Let the world's riches, which dispersed lie,
   Contract into a span.

So strength first made a way;
Then beauty flow'd, then wisdom, honour, pleasure:
When almost all was out, God made a stay,
Perceiving that alone of all his treasure
   Rest in the bottom lay.

For if I should (said he)
Bestow this jewel also on my creature,
He would adore my gifts instead of me,
And rest in Nature, not the God of Nature:
   So both should losers be.

Yet let him keep the rest,
But keep them with repining restlessness:
Let him be rich and weary, that at least,
If goodness lead him not, yet weariness
   May toss him to my breast.[14]

This poem by George Herbert is called *The Pulley* and it suggests how the denial of rest is a means of drawing us to a greater rest: our heart is restless, says St Augustine addressing God, until it rests in thee.[15] Tied down to even the fullest mere ego-life the heart is 'rich and weary'. The rest that alone can satisfy is in the God of nature, not in nature. To achieve this, it is necessary to be detached from the hopes and fears that present themselves as though absolute. Each fear is the prospect of a death in a story told by Scheherazade, but the death is an illusion and an enchantment because it is not ultimately important. It will pass away with time and another will take its place. All that will remain is the immortal soul as it has been made or marred by its terrestrial life. Even the final death of earthly life is not to be avoided at the cost of hurt to the soul; much less is the pain of hopes lost, fears come true, to be avoided at that cost.

   This rest of soul in the Divine is something that is open to it before the death of earthly life. It is not simply a matter of moral conformity – that, as well as pleasure-seeking, can be a tangle of anxious hopes and fears. A couple of analogies can suggest how the soul's resting in the Divine differs from ego-life. Imagine a tourist from a western country visiting an African country. His anxieties swing about looking for what they can fasten on. Is the water bottled, do the lavatories flush, will I catch the train, will I be embarrassed? There is a fragility in his condition that comes from his fears. And there is a superficiality that comes from his hopes. Will the company give me that new car? Can I get what I want for breakfast here? Will it be sunny all the time? As with Parkinson's law that work expands to fill the time available for its completion, so these hopes and fears do not so much diminish when the outcomes they claim are accomplished as look around for a new place to dwell. That is to say that they are an aspect of the soul more essentially than they are a state of affairs in the world requiring attention. The soul is focused on things that pass away: the western tourist betrays, in his eyes and gait, a lack of depth and steadiness. He is in striking contrast to the native African: unworried about the past or the future, the African is content simply to enjoy and accept what life brings. His dignified, calm serenity is reflected in the steadiness of his gait and the limpid sureness of his eyes. By all this, I do not imply that the west has nothing to teach the African or that lying in the sun is the cure to all our spiritual ills: I simply offer two images of the two kinds of life – ego-life and soul-life. They are presented as images in a poem might be, not as human embodiments of good and ill.

Another way of seeing the difference between the two kinds of life is to imagine two kinds of company on a sea voyage. The first is very anxious that you should be well satisfied: she comes and wakes you up in the morning to make sure you don't miss breakfast; she chatters to you during breakfast in case you feel lonely; she whisks the breakfast things away from you as you are eating the final mouthful of toast so that you don't feel you have to do the washing up . . . and so on. The other has a quiet calm radiance: in her presence you feel that there is goodness in the world; she radiates cheerfulness; she is completely reliable – if anything needs to be done she will do it; she allows God to be present to you. The first gives you the benefit of her anxiety, the second of her presence. There are various assumptions underlying the sort of attention given by the first shipboard companion – it is assumed that attention to real or imaginary desires is the best thing for you: *they* are important. The other companion is saying something different: *you* are important, *I* am important. She is refusing to submit the dignity and peace of people to the tyranny of their passing desires. The sea voyage can represent life's journey, the companion what our heart chooses, what it treasures: false or true values, fretfulness or peace.

It is claimed, then, that there is life beyond the death of ego-life and that this life is available before the death of earthly life. If this claim is accepted, the yoghurt-abhorring persona can be let go of in the confidence of the existence of a more fundamental person. The source of the authority of this claim is Christian faith, which proclaims the resurrection of Christ and the sharing of the believer in that resurrection. Our 'life is hid with Christ in God'.[16] This participation in His life is not simply the promise of a freshly yoghurt-abhorring existence after death – a consummation in the future of what went before. It is a breaking out of time (as a butterfly from a chrysalis) and a liberation from the fears and hopes contingent on it. The sort of confidence it offers is not the kind offered by the prospect of a cheerful meal in the evening which helps one get through the day's work. It is the confidence of eternal life, which because it is eternal is in some sense there in the present, our partial window into the eternal. The present is like a prism, showing us the single, all-illuminated white light of eternity, but showing it refracted in the multiplicity of colours of timely and spatial events. But it is possible to be aware – through a glass darkly – of that light. The means of awareness of it is faith. St John writes: 'Whatever is born of God overcomes the world; and this is the victory that overcomes the world, our faith'.[17] We might paraphrase this: 'from an eternal source comes something that makes nugatory the passing hopes and fears that are bound by time: we have access to this eternal source that can make the anxieties associated with these hopes and fears nugatory through faith'. We shall go on to consider the journey of the soul to the sweetness hidden in tribulation from the point of view of its acquisition of faith.

CHAPTER FIVE

ULTIMATE REINSURANCE

Faith in God's love for us
enables us to love others

Faith gives the possibility of escaping from false values and finding true life. This chapter will examine the way in which we are liberated to love others truly by faith in God's love for us. It will also discuss how faith grows gradually towards this strength in loving. In the context of this power of faith and the concomitant importance of growth towards it, tribulation can be seen in a joyful light if it plays a part in that growth.

When an insurer takes on big risks, it is usual for him to reinsure himself with another insurer so that if he has to pay out an exceptionally large amount, he can reclaim it. There comes a point, however, where someone has to take the risk. It is infeasible to have a system in which it is absolutely impossible for funds to be unavailable in the end. Something analogous occurs in the field of human relations. A person may have to deal with someone whose attitude he finds affronting and alienating. However, he can cope with this because he knows that he is supported and understood by a friend. This friend in turn knows he can count on the love and sympathy of his wife. The wife may be sure of the care and concern of her father. However, there is nothing within the network of relations that can absolutely guarantee that discord, distrust and lack of love will not grow up. Perhaps the love will survive on its own the lifetime of the people involved: there is no guarantee, however, that it will be successfully passed on to their children. In any case, it remains at risk from accidents of circumstance: illness, separation or death can break a link and damage the security.

This security depends on a particular desire being fulfilled: that of being valued and supported by another person. A perennial symbol of this is being invited to share food. Can this be done without hope of some kind of reciprocation? It would seem that we need to be able to assume that somebody will do it for us. There is another option, however, the only one which can offer ultimate reinsurance – faith. This is set out in the gospel:

> When you give a dinner or a banquet, do not invite your friends or your brothers or your kinsmen or rich neighbours, lest they also invite you in return, and you be repaid. But when you give a feast, invite the poor, the maimed, the lame, the blind, and you will be blessed, because they cannot repay you. You will be repaid at the resurrection of the just.[1]

If we have faith we are not finally dependent on the network of human support: we are ultimately reinsured. The underwriting of the willingness to forego reciprocation appears to relate to the future: 'you will be repaid'. There is more to it, however. The exhortation is to unselfish love: aim, it says, to give. If you are inviting those who will return the favour, it is likely to be not so much giving as a mercantile proposition, or at least a good bet. It is self-love, rather than love for another for their own sake. The poor, the maimed, the lame and the blind, however, can only be loved for their own sake, since they cannot repay, so if you love them it really will be love. And, in the words of the beloved disciple, 'God is love, and he who abides in love abides in God, and God abides in him'.[2] So anyone who is giving without expectation of earthly return (in which we must include feeling good about giving) is already in the presence of God.

So from God himself, from his presence, comes the strength to set aside a preoccupation with the hope of human support. The difficulty for actually living this is really acquiring confidence in him in our personal dealings. Here, for example, is an emotionally maimed person who, the general experience suggests, will respond with coldness and even bitterness to openness and tenderness. How is one to go on caring? The Christian answer is faith: faith that the resurrection of Christ witnesses to a life that is beyond death; faith that in the scriptures is the assurance of God's love for us; faith that in the eucharist we can see his presence. We can see the results of this faith in the assurance God's love gives to saints and faithful Christians. Faith is the confidence that unselfish love is repaid and that we are loved by God. It believes that what is given is received in a spiritual reality that has more substance than material reality. The difficulty, however, with faith is the absence of material assurance. The consecrated elements of the eucharist give us God materially, but they do not, in their material aspect, give us the faith by which we know God in them. And there is the lack of material return from all those dinner guests.

It is worth asking how it could be otherwise. God is the source of the universe, utterly greater than anything confined by time and space. We cannot expect to have him reduced to something we can probe and manipulate in our anxiety for reassurance. There is a parallel in human love. The difference between someone who invites us to dinner and expresses appreciation for us with a view to getting something out of us and someone who does the same out of pure love is, in the end, something that cannot be pinned down simply in terms of evidence. In principle any token of love could be insincere. Even the most loving person can only go on offering tokens of love – in the end you have to believe him.

Friends can be hugged, however. There is a certain rest and security possible in terrestrial relations that would be grasped from the ultimate reinsurer who yet does not seem to admit to tangibility. Where do you take your rest if your meat and drink is what the ultimate lover wants? The answer is bleak:

> Foxes have holes, and birds of the air have nests; but the
> Son of Man has nowhere to lay his head.[3]

This is the One whose meat and drink is to do the will of the Source of all security.[4] To follow him appears to offer less security than is given to lesser creatures than man. The truth is, however, not that it is less security, but that it is on a higher plane. The foxes and birds have, as it were, security in single figures: followers of Christ have nothing in single figures, but have it a hundredfold, even in this life. His own reinsurance paid out with resurrection from the dead and majesty at the right hand of God. His eternal presence is available to Christians. He offers us a transcendent, not a terrestrial security.

Faith enables the acceptance of the bleakness and darkness of earthly life, and the endurance of darkness leads to great light. In particular it enables the acceptance of the superficially unrewarding nature of the poor, the maimed, the lame and the blind. In a sense this is the whole of humanity: all fallen, all unable to make a perfect return of love. In this way, the network of human relations is reinsured: absolute dependence is placed not in them, but in the divine. A detachment is possible, not in the bad sense of not being responsive to the needs of others, but in the good sense of not having to have a certain response from them in order to be happy. That makes it possible to go on loving the poor in sensitivity, the maimed of heart, the lame in good works and the blind to the needs of others.

Faith too makes desires for other things relative. It liberates us from a compulsive addiction to our desires being fulfilled, because it enables us to live in our deeper selves. It frees us from the anxiety that attachment to the time-bound creates: anxiety about the past and future does not have the last, binding word because the affections are set on the eternal. In the journey to the blessed land where tribulation is sweet there may, however, be growing-pains: faith reaches towards serenity. The presence of anxieties does not mean an absence of faith, but that its work is not finished. Hopkins' poem *Peace* expresses this well:

> When will you ever, Peace, wild wooddove, shy wings
>   shut,
> Your round me roving end, and under be my boughs?
> When, when, Peace, will you, Peace? – I'll not play
>   hypocrite
> To my own heart: I yield you do come sometimes;
>   but
> That piecemeal peace is poor peace. What pure peace
>   allows

Alarms of wars, the daunting wars, the death of it?

O surely, reaving Peace, my Lord should leave in lieu
Some good! And so he does leave Patience exquisite,
That plumes to Peace thereafter. And when Peace here
   does house
He comes with work to do, he does not come to coo,
              He comes to brood and sit.[5]

Peace comes with the knowledge of being absolutely loved by God which gives an inner joy that cannot be disturbed by other troubles. Faith is our means to this knowledge. Peace sometimes nonetheless seems to be flying around, fretting us by not coming to roost – or only doing so sometimes, allowing at others great disquiet. When the Lord is 'reaving' – carrying off – peace it is natural to feel we should be given something instead. We are: we are given patience. This is the virtue that tends to peace. We act as though we are at peace, despite being troubled, and this leads to it. When peace does come, it comes 'with work to do', not simply to be enjoyed. The work is bringing into conformity with it all that is not aligned with it – all those attitudes that deny its presence in their fretfulness.

This poem speaks to us of the life of faith if we think of peace as that state in which we have a sense of God's presence and love, and patience as that attitude we take when we act in the conviction of these, but without awareness of them. This patience is taking things well: taking the blows we receive in our attempts to love as veiling God's love to us. The development of this virtue of patience, faith that God's love is behind our troubles so they should not agitate us, leads us towards peace: awareness of his presence. This awareness, when it comes, will tell us what is and is not conducive to that presence filling us more, and its work is to change what doesn't help to what does.

Faith is a grasping of the ungraspable, of the ultimate meaning that makes everything all right. It is the seed of the knowledge that comes to us not through the working of our minds, but from beyond time and space. Faith and prayer,

which reaches beyond time and space, are natural partners
and George Herbert's poem *Prayer* speaks of both:

> Prayer the Church's banquet, Angels' age,
>> God's breath in man returning to his birth,
>> The soul in paraphrase, heart in pilgrimage,
> The Christian plummet sounding heav'n and earth;
>
> Engine against th'Almighty, sinners' tower,
>> Reversed thunder, Christ-side-piercing spear,
>> The six-days' world-transposing in an hour,
> A kind of tune, which all things hear and fear;
>
> Softness, and peace, and joy, and love, and bliss,
>> Exalted Manna, gladness of the best,
>> Heaven in ordinary, man well dressed,
> The milky way, the bird of Paradise,
>
>> Church-bells beyond the stars heard, the soul's blood,
>> The land of spices; something understood.[6]

Faith, like the prayer it engenders, reaches out to what the
mind cannot grasp, and becomes itself a higher kind of
understanding. Earth and heaven are both measured by it. It
is the life of God in mankind. It tells us what our essential
nature is: gives us a paraphrase of our soul until such time as
it is revealed in heaven. It is the map of our heart's pilgrimage.
It is our means of grasping God. It changes the way we look
at the creation: it reveals the ultimate harmony behind all that
happens. It makes possible a gentleness and softness because
in its light life is known not to depend on the harsh defence
of some merely terrestrial interest. It is a well of joy because
it sees the life of heaven hidden in ordinary existence. With
it life cannot be merely mundane because it has celestial
echoes ('church-bells beyond the stars heard') and is tinged
with the exotic ('the land of spices'). Above all, faith gives life
meaning: faith, like prayer, is 'something understood'.

In this context tribulation can seem sweet. St James writes
'Count it all joy, my brethren, when you meet various trials,
for you know that the testing of your faith produces

steadfastness'.[7] If faith has reached a certain vigour then 'various trials' make it more steadfast – strengthen it by exercising it. As Blake says, 'Damn braces, bless relaxes'.[8] A lack of merely mundane consolation sharpens the awareness of spiritual reality. The wind of tribulation that might extinguish a feeble faith fans the flames of a fiercer faith. That effect (not the tribulation) is a cause of joy since faith transfigures life, casting upon it a heavenly halo.

Such a life is not only joyful, it is liberated. It is free from the self-guarding need to see to one's own insurance; it gives the assurance of love and frees one to love. The person with faith is free to embrace their fellows because they don't have to be covering their back. They are not the slave to any limited objective: nothing on earth is ultimately important to them. That means they are able to work for the good of others without preoccupations. They are free of concern about self: they know the very hairs of their head are counted.[9] The difference between the reception a person with deep faith can give others and that which a person with less faith can give is suggested by imagining two invitations to tea. One is from a lady who has taken great trouble to lay out an elaborate spread on an exquisite china service and has arranged the finest chairs for you to sit on. When you arrive she is most insistent that you partake of the good things. As the social occasion develops, however, you become aware of a certain tension. You soon realise that it is a matter of the most anxious importance how you handle the china: it may well be that you will break it. When you come to sit down the question is raised (perhaps only implicitly) of whether you might not damage the chair. This hostess's heart is set on the world and her particular stake in it in china and furniture: she cannot be free of her concern because she is not sure that there would be anything worthwhile if this was taken from her. By contrast the hostess with deeper faith is concerned with drawing out her guest who is made to feel at home and relaxed. She has an intuitive grasp of how to set free the very best in them and this is her reward. She knows that in the measure she gives it will be returned to her, pressed down and running over. The thought of crockery and chairs never crosses her mind.

We have examined how faith enables people to reach out to their fellows. It is also a way of accepting what doesn't seem to have any positive value at all: this too merits consideration.

CHAPTER SIX

TRUSTING

*The joy of being loved by God
can mean more than pain*

The most essential message of faith is that we are loved by God. As we have discussed in the last chapter, this message can free us to love others. It can also give strength to accept what would otherwise be affronting. If we have faith that God loves us, and faith in his providence, then the apparently senseless and even cruel can be reinterpreted as part of a message of love. Jesus crucified was perfectly loved by his Father. In our own lives faith can see love where otherwise there is only meaninglessness. It is a question of trusting God's goodness. This goodness is transcendent and eternal, not temporal and material. Therefore, although it is present and expressed in the good things of creation, its essence is beyond them. What we trust when we trust God's goodness is not primarily the things of creation (for example, that it won't rain if this suits us) but the Creator himself and his love for us. The deeper this trust the more we are drawn into a blessed state of mutual love, since our love for God grows as we become more sure of his love for us. On the other hand, placing an absolute trust in the contingent things of creation is likely to have an opposite (souring) effect – we put our trust in a particular outcome and are embittered when it doesn't come about, because we haven't listened to God's message of love which is not in the words we chose for him. It follows that changing from the latter to the former attitude is a very good thing. If frustration of our desires with regard to created things (which we can call tribulation) is the means by which we learn to trust more and more in the right (love-engendering, life-giving) place, then it may be called sweet. This chapter explores the faith that grasps God's love for us even in tribulation and is more directed towards its proper object (purified, made steadfast) by that very tribulation.

An analogy from personal relations may help to make clear

how faith can see God's love for us in what would otherwise be affronting. Suppose one is driving to work and one sees in the driving mirror a colleague or a workmate in his car. Suppose him to be a person who is great fun to work with: he has a generous ebullient personality that can take everything that comes his way in a light-hearted and merry spirit. Suppose also that this spirit is so obviously full of good will that it is impossible to take anything he says other than in a friendly way: knowing him well one knows that his aim is to spread happiness. Just after one has noticed him in the mirror he overtakes. As he pulls out, rude fingers emerge from the sunroof and wave in victory. This is no more than something to laugh about when you both get to work. Imagine, however that on another occasion it is a stranger that our cheerful friend overtakes. It so happens that his car is exactly the same model and colour as one's own. It is possible that he will not find it so funny. We can see the fingers emerging from the sunroof as 'the slings and arrows of outrageous fortune'[1] – at least insofar as they are humiliating. The person who knows the waver as a source of merry fun can be seen as one who has faith. The driver who has no grasp of the intention of his overtaker and is affronted is like the person who has no faith when events humiliate him.

St Paul put this differently: 'We know that in everything God works for good with those who love him, who are called according to his purpose'.[2] It may be objected that being overtaken is not painful really, and therefore not a sufficient metaphor for tribulation. That is true, and yet a considerable part of what is experienced as pain is really the concomitant affront and humiliation. Turn that into merry fun and the pain may be bearable. Imagine a much-loved child making the first present of his life. He jumps into his mother's lap to make it. Unfortunately the buckle of his shoe sticks painfully into her leg. Which is she going to notice: the pain or the present? In both this image and that of being overtaken, the key point is the knowledge of the intention of the person behind what is happening. Faith is the knowledge of God's loving intention. God is behind or (better) within everything that happens, so faith means seeing everything that happens to us as being ordained or allowed for our good. That good may not be immediately comprehensible to us. It may be difficult for us to see it because we are obstinate in wanting another particular good. This may be a good that needs to be left behind in order for us to be open to what is really good for us. An extreme example of this would be an addiction to the pleasure of taking heroin. Yet obstinately wanting anything which is not the good that God has chosen for us (and since God loves us he can only choose good for us) might be seen as an addiction.

The attitude that faith develops is one of taking everything well. It is an attitude to the whole of life and its ultimate meaning that has an analogy on the inter-personal level. The person who never takes offence, who is always ready to see the good intentions in other people's actions is analogous to the one who has faith. This is only an analogy, not an identity. A person of this sort is Jane Bennett in Jane Austen's *Pride and Prejudice*. In the novel there is a certain amount of irony directed towards her blindly trusting attitude, which contrasts with that of her sharp-witted sister Elizabeth. Nonetheless such an attitude is preferable to the opposite one, analogous to faithlessness, which is quick to take offence, always finding reasons for mistrust. It is capable of evoking a noble response from others who, not shown such trust, would show a less pleasant side of their nature. The analogy is incomplete because total trust in others is imprudent, and God's goodness – unlike that of those of whom Jane Bennett thinks so well – is absolutely trustworthy. The analogy is at its best in the connection between the way showing trust in someone can bring out a noble side of their nature, and the way faith in God is rewarded; for example, the faith that Abraham shows when he responds to the Lord's words, 'Go from your country and your kindred and your father's house to the land that I will show you'.[3] Abraham is rewarded by being made the father of a great nation. An appeal to God's better nature, as it were, always works, since in him there is no darkness. St Thérèse gave this attitude a bold expression. When she was suffering, she said, she paid God all sorts of compliments and he didn't know what to do with her any more.[4] She urges an attitude of complete trust in God's providence: one should be as a child asleep in its father's arms. This childlike faith, which can so change tribulation, is very far removed from immaturity. It is a matter of being childlike in the right way and adult in the right way. The proper direction for being adult is outward. We shouldn't cast ourselves into 'the glass of outer weariness' with childish impetuosity. That is, we should exercise an adult restraint and maturity about what we take for our enjoyment: it would be wrong, for example, to eat only ice cream because it is 'nice'. That would be a misplacing of our childlike instincts. Inwardly, however, we should trust as a child, opening our eyes to God's love. Here a mistakenly 'adult' attitude would be a cynical guardedness, refusing to give or trust on the pretext of prudence. It would be a hardness where the 'tender eyes grow all unkind'.

Jesus identifies the proper way to be adult and to be childlike when he tells his disciples to be as wise as serpents and as innocent as doves.[5] We should have a serpent-like wariness of our tendency to give an absolute value to any precarious pleasure. St Augustine tells the story of how, on his path towards faith, he was preparing with some anxiety a speech in praise of the emperor when he came across a drunken beggar. The thought came to him that the kind of pleasure of success that he aspired to was in reality of the same kind as the merriment of the beggar. His mind was befuddled and the pleasure he was seeking was unstable.[6] This thought was the seed in his mind of the serpent-like aspect of faith, the faith that would grow till it could see the childishness of merely worldly ambitions.

The dove-like, or childlike aspect of faith is shown in the response of the believer to what happens to him and not in a naïve credulity about the power of the merely passing to give him satisfaction. He takes everything that happens in the best possible way, trusting God as a child trusts his father to do what is best for him. This doesn't mean, of course, being passive when something positive can be done. It means rather that when tribulation comes there is no withdrawal into bitterness or an unnecessarily defensive attitude. In fact this attitude is more likely to lead to a positively active response than a more consciously hard-nosed one. The trust in God means that one is not going to give up on life. Imagine, for example, someone whose birthday has been forgotten by his fellows. He had expected, as was usual when somebody's birthday came round, that a bottle of wine would be pro-duced and that he would be toasted. A falsely adult attitude would say inwardly 'well, they don't care about me, I shall be colder and more wary towards them: you won't find me going out of my way to remember when their birthdays come round'. The childlike attitude (which could, in another sense, be called more grown-up) just accepts the poor memory of the others as the way things are (no more a matter for taking offence at than the sun going behind a cloud) and the person gifted with it goes out and buys a bottle of wine and invites his fellows to celebrate his birthday with him. This attitude might appear more selfish and the other one more self-effacing, but in reality it affirms – and brings out – the good will of others while the other, in overlooking the possibility of their positive response once invited, denies their potential good will. It is an attitude of faith in the possibilities of good in life. It believes that if God does not bestow one good, that is because he is bestowing another. Faith that one is loved by God leads to an openness to everything that is good in life.

So much of the limitation that people impose on them-selves comes from a defensiveness that generalises from a negative experience. An obvious example is someone who has been snubbed in a friendship (or thinks they have been) and is thereafter wary and untrusting with others, denying themselves the possibility of friendship. A faith-filled attitude would accept the snub (even if it were indubitably real) as not contradicting the ultimate fact of one's being loved by God. It will go on being open therefore to what God's love has to offer, both directly (as apprehended, for example, in prayer and spiritual reading) and through others. This attitude will in fact tend to encourage the friendship of others. One might say, to reappropriate a word that is sometimes used as a justification for mean-spiritedness, that it is a realistic attitude. It accepts the real goodness of God and therefore sees everything good that life has to offer, eschewing the paranoic fantasies of an attitude falsely thought of as realistic, the sort of attitude that says, 'I know what they're like, you've got to watch them, you know...' It is childlike in that it is always fresh and ready for the next good thing. It doesn't take the little point of darkness that has come into one's life in the past and stretch it out into a line that runs through the present, scoring out its joy.

Faith, however, is more than an attitude that enables one to make the best of things, since it is open not only to whatever is good in things, but also to the absolute goodness of the Creator of all things. This openness is such a good thing that it is worth selling any number of little pearls to buy this pearl of great price.[7] A willingness to accept inevitable suffering, and even to think it sweet, is understandable in the light of this fact. This is because when one is suffering, the option of fastening onto unstable and transitory goods as though they were absolute (being a child in the wrong sort of way) can hardly exist: the only sort of consolation that can help is from the God of all consolation and, denied anything less, one can only turn trustingly to him (being a child in the right sort of way). In this way suffering, rightly accepted, can strengthen and mature faith. Faith is our means of knowing God who is greater than anything that can be grasped by the senses: when suffering denies us any (sensual) consolation, we are in a position where we have to rely on the (sensually) obscure knowledge of faith. The more we undertake that reliance, the more we are trusting God: the more we trust him, the more we achieve the openness to him that is so valuable. The more open we are to him, the more we grow in knowledge of him and are strengthened by our closeness to him. This spiritual strength can be manifested on a physical level, as it was in the case of St Maximilian Kolbe who outlived all the others with whom he was placed in a Nazi starvation bunker. Its source is otherworldly: it is a strength that does not come from natural expedients for cheering oneself up, such as drink and the complimentary conversation of compliant companions, it comes from eternity. A way of understanding how it is communicated is to think of faith as a turning inwards, in Yeats' words, a gazing 'in thine own heart', and to see this as an intercourse with the immortal part of oneself. This immortal self is independent of anything that can happen within the matrix of space and time: it therefore cannot be harmed against its will by whatever tribulation is afflicting the person. It is therefore a source of inalienable strength and serenity, which, as the dwelling place of the eternal God, it can communicate to the extent that the person turns to it from 'the glass of outer weariness'. The stronger faith is, the more complete is this turning or conversion. The more complete the conversion, the less one reacts with bitterness and malice against the affronts to the self as that self is experienced within time and space, and the more one reacts with the radiation of the inner goodness that is eternally and inwardly communicated. In other words, the more faith one has the less one is a victim (in the sense of being made nastier by them) of the things that happen to one and the more loving and forgiving one is, qualities that are of supreme value both in this world and the next.

An understanding of this process of the maturation of faith through reliance on God in suffering can make sense of Job's reaction to misfortune: 'The Lord gave, and the Lord has taken away; blessed be the name of the Lord'.[8] It also explains how St Thérèse can write to her sister Céline of a third person that her soul is not yet matured because she has not yet suffered much. Suffering, as she sees it, is a means of reaching one's own depths. One might almost say it drives one into them – if it is allowed to, if it is trustingly accepted as being allowed (or ordained) by a most loving God, never for the bad in it, but for this most treasurable good. If this is sought, this deepening of faith, then other good things follow.[9] To the seeker of the kingdom of heaven are given good things that are not the focus of the search but rather signs that it is progressing. There is first the ability discussed above to escape the malign influence of the past on the present. The person with a deep faith does not cut themselves off because they have suffered. They can be free, not of trouble, but of those pestiferent troubles that are caused by redundant reactions to troubles. Then, faith brings confidence. I have heard it said that Christianity undermines people's confidence by making them think of what they are doing wrong whereas what most people need is a boosting of their confidence. The analysis of people's need is correct, but the judgement of what Christianity does is superficial. The reason people so often lack confidence is that they look for their security in what is external to their truest selves: 'the glass of outer weariness'. 'If I were as clever/beautiful/energetic as so-and-so, then I would believe in myself more' is a wish that even if it were fulfilled would not bring the desired results – the confidence would still remain vulnerable to competition. Christianity offers a confidence that is not based on cleverness, beauty or energy. It is not even based on doing what is right: it is based on the opposite of sin (which it does undermine) – faith.

Faith gives confidence because, as it deepens, it leads one more and more into that area where the basic reality is one's absolute acceptance by God. In the light of the wonderful fact of being so loved, whether or not one is esteemed as clever or admired as beautiful is as unimportant as the opinion of someone with no money to the market-researcher. The creator of beauty, the fount of wisdom offers – gratis – unconditional affirmation: what need is there cravenly to crave that merely mediated by creatures? One can say with the Master, 'I do not receive glory from men'.[10] This is not to say that people of faith are coldly indifferent to the opinion of others, just that their confidence is not in thrall to it. This absolute acceptance or unconditional affirmation is not dependent on goodness, or good deeds (as affirmation by others may be, even if it is not dependent on cleverness or beauty). It depends only on openness – openness in faith to the goodness of God and, in the confidence that faith gives, to the reality of one's state. It is a false, and therefore insecure, confidence that depends on cloaking with flattery or self-deceit one's failings. True confidence is the laying open of them to God in the conviction that he is able to heal them. Faith gives this confidence because it believes in his love. It enables one to be confident not because one is good but because God is good. St Thérèse wrote of going to God with empty hands:[11] his goodness, not her deeds were to be her justification. It is the same for everyone. Faith shows the redundance of defensiveness, the futility of self-justification: it gives, instead, the courage to look openly and realistically at God's goodness, at the good things that life offers and at one's own weakness without being discouraged by it. The man of faith's confidence is not in his accomplishments or deeds, but at a much deeper level, in the immortal God who dwells within his soul and – at his good pleasure – does good through him. By contrast, the person who has placed their confidence in competitive accomplishment is vulnerable – like the man who was a top racing cyclist and upon retirement couldn't cope with the reduced level of public esteem and took to smashing up restaurants when he didn't get the attention he wanted from the waiter. This is the 'glass of outer weariness' taking its revenge. The man of faith doesn't live on the surface like this, but where the Creator of life himself is always renewing his life.

Faith gives a rootedness in the eternal that transforms the way trouble and tribulation are accepted, so that they can even become partners in the only growth that matters – growth towards the eternal. The theological virtue of hope changes the way a person is affected by fear of tribulation in the future as well as anguish about tribulation in the past. It can liberate the listener from the enchantment of the tale told by Scheherazade, and free his soul from being rapt by what has been heard and wrapped fearfully in the question of what happens next. The next chapter will begin the examination of how it, like faith, can work for the transformation of tribulation, co-opting it in the quest for the transcendent.

CHAPTER SEVEN

THE LOCKED-AWAY MIND

The pain of not living in the present

Faith looks beyond the tale told by Scheherazade. What is seen by its light gives strength to undertake its imperative, the love of others. Its trust sees benevolence in and beyond every circumstance. Its openness to heavenly light can transform the tribulation and struggle of life. The theological virtue of hope is its companion-in-arms. We have seen (in Chapter Five) how through faith it is possible to escape from false values, from treating anything in the created order as though it were absolute. It enables the transfer of trust from a particular thing to the eternal God. Hope (in the theological sense) works like this too. Through this hope it is possible to escape from the false values of time, from the temporary to the eternal. It liberates the soul from the unreality of living in the past and the uncertainty of living in the future. These shadows of life are replaced with communion with God. Points of time, past or to pass, are not treated as though they were absolute. Eternity, and not the vanishings of time, becomes the focus. With the strength of this hope, tribulation can be borne. It can even help to sharpen the focus on the eternal by diverting the soul from the evanescent to the everlasting.

Where hope in God is weak, on the other hand, Scheherazade's siren song can tie up the person in hopes and fears that are bound by time – aspirations which, as Beckett understood, if fulfilled, only satisfy the shadow of a past self. A new crisis in the story is then anticipated: new hopes, new fears replace those that had affected the person. To one enchanted by Scheherazade's tale, it would seem that this is chronic and endemic to the human condition: how can man live without his sights set on something in the future? Yet once the sights are locked onto it, the mind is locked away: it reacts positively or negatively not to what is present, what is real, but to the spectre of what may or may not be. The future casts a sort of shadow of unreality over the present. The past can do the same, regret or nostalgia blocking openness to what is going on, the mind locked onto the things that are no more. This chapter examines this aspect of the human condition, the locked-away mind, and argues that hope of the theological kind is radically different from the hope that wants something that comes and goes as time passes. Theological hope, it claims, can liberate mankind both from the tension and unreality that preoccupation with this hope brings and from the frustration and unreality that preoccupation with the past brings.

Both these temporal preoccupations absorb the soul on the level of ego-life, that is the life that is mortal, that passes away. Hope operates in the inner life that faith brings to notice. This is the life that is of God, eternal life, which escapes the caging in of time. We shall consider the nature of the caging first and then reflect on how theological hope offers a way beyond it.

It is a necessary part of human life to think about the past with a view to gaining an understanding that will make possible prudent decisions. This cannot be considered as being trapped in the past. Similarly to reflect sensibly about what needs to be done in the future does not go against the spirit of the injunction to take no care for the morrow.[1] Hamlet correctly identifies the purposes of Providence when he says

> Sure He that made us with such large discourse,
> Looking before and after, gave us not
> That capability and godlike reason
> To fust in us unus'd.[2]

The 'large discourse, looking before and after' is given to us as a servant, however, and not as a master. Man is intended to be joyfully free of pain from the past and anxiousness about tomorrow. Even the glad aspect of his involvement in the past and future – happy memories and eager anticipation – is not good enough for him: he is meant for the more real and substantial joy of the present moment. In his post-lapsarian condition, however, his tendency is to incomplete mastery of his 'large discourse'. Instead of turning to God who is in the present (man's point of contact with the eternal) and placing his hope in his love for him, man tends to look for his meaning in the past or future. The mistake is not thinking about them, but expecting to be satisfied by them, when they lack the reality that only the present can give.

There is an analogy with what was observed about the difference between the adult and the childish way of looking at 'the glass of outer weariness'. The adult approaches it prudently, seeing it for what it is, something that is unable to give absolute satisfaction, and the childish person (not the child necessarily) has a naïve view of what can be gained from it. Similarly the adult will reflect on the past and future prudently for the sake of wise decisions, but not in the expectation of finding present or fulfilling joy in them. Just as the wise and mature person looks, not into the 'glass of outer weariness', but inwardly into their own heart with a childlike trust to find the tree of joy, so they hope for bliss, not in the insubstantiality of time not present, but in the moment they are living in, where God is. They will look at the present as a dove and at the past and future as a serpent. Another way of putting all this would be to say that the wise person seeks perfect fulfilment in God himself rather than in his creation in time and space.

The nature of this wise hope may be made clearer by contrast by considering examples of people looking at the present, unwisely, with the eyes of a serpent. Characteristic of this gaze is a corroding cynicism, the devil's version of the virtue of prudence. The cynicism may come from a mind locked away either in the past or the future. Miss Havisham, in Dickens' novel *Great Expectations*, is the epitome of one locked away in the past. She lives in a room where there is 'no glimpse of daylight'[3] – the vitality that can only be found in the present. Her hope is obstinately placed in what she knows can offer her no joy: the finery of the wedding day on which she was abandoned. She embodies a splendour arrested in the past. Dickens' description of her draws attention to the fatuity of trying to keep the spontaneity (and potential joy) of the past by keeping the marks of the outward signs of that spontaneity, unfinished things:

> She was dressed in rich materials – satins, and lace, and
> silks – all of white. Her shoes were white. And she had
> a long white veil dependent from her hair, and she had
> bridal flowers in her hair, but her hair was white. Some
> bright jewels sparkled on her neck and on her hands,
> and some other jewels lay sparkling on the table.
> Dresses, less splendid than the dress she wore, and half-
> packed trunks, were scattered about. She had not quite
> finished dressing, for she had but one shoe on – the
> other was on the table near her hand – her veil was but
> half arranged, her watch and chain were not put on, and
> some lace for her bosom lay with those trinkets, and with
> her handkerchief, and gloves, and some flowers, and a
> prayer-book, all confusedly heaped about the looking-
> glass.[4]

Physically, the jewels are real, but the joy that they symbol-ise
is unreal, locked in the past. The half-finished things are,
physically, unfinished, but the life that they symbolise is
finished, is in the past. The boy observing realises that what
looked white, because it should have been white, is faded:

> I saw that everything within my view which ought to be
> white, had been white long ago, and had lost its lustre,
> and was faded and yellow. I saw that the bride within the
> bridal dress had withered like the dress, and like the
> flowers, and had no brightness left but the brightness of
> her sunken eyes.[5]

The fadedness is the fadedness of (in Tennyson's words)
'a day that is dead'.[6] It is significant that the only brightness in
the room is the brightness of Miss Havisham's eyes. Symbolically, these are the present moment, the single point of reality
in the scene; they are the life without which the past would
not have even its chimeric existence. They are the life that is
prostituted to its sordid unreality. They are the human soul
enslaved to the past. This enslavement precludes openness to

the healing influence of other people: Miss Havisham tells the boy, 'I have done with men and women'.[7] There is a tiny ray of hope for Miss Havisham, however: not in men and women, but in the child whom she is here meeting for the first time. At this point it is only the hope of a real hope, one that is freed from the past. Here it expresses itself in her wish that the boy play. The circumstances could not be more unpropitious than they are for his doing so. This is an indication of the extent to which Miss Havisham has cut herself off from the source of spontaneity, the present. Nonetheless, her very request for him to play is an acknowledgement of her need to re-establish contact with the present, with spontaneity (and by implication, God). It starts a relationship with him which, although it begins by being exploitative, ends with her acknowledging her need for forgiveness and her desire to do something good for him. Her wanting the child to play is the seed of her redemption. The spontaneity that she hoped for from him eventually becomes her own so that she can love, and to love is to be saved. The serpent and the dove exchange places.

The exemplification of the mind locked away in the future will be taken not from literature, but from advertising. This is appropriate, since the sort of unhealthy engagement with the future that we are considering is not something that occurs spontaneously (indeed, lack of spontaneity is the heart of its weakness), but which is worked up by deliberate influence of the kind that advertising exerts. A certain kind of advertising can be seen as the spiritual reading of materialism. What prayerful reading does to put the soul in touch with God, this advertising does to lock it onto the material world and the relatively unreal hope of future (and timebound) acquisition. The move from the former to the latter process and the difference between them is articulated by the prophet Jeremiah: 'My people have committed two evils: they have forsaken me, the fountain of living waters, and hewed out cisterns for themselves, broken cisterns, that can hold no water'.[8] The heart that hopes in God is perpetually refreshed, but the heart that is set on worldly goods in the future is looking for refreshment from a broken cistern. The very contradiction of hoping for the vitality of the present from what has no present reality is caught in the advertising slogan: 'The future. Now.' The mind is locked onto something that has no existence and told that it does exist. The tendency to set the soul on future time that advertising encourages is imaged in the names given to products (itself a form of advertising): clothes are 'next', snacks are 'sooner'. This is a kind of spiritual hysteria which is unable to rest in the present, but spuriously hopes for a future qualitatively different from it, a future to which it will bring the restlessness that George Herbert describes in *The Pulley*, a restlessness that can no more be changed by being moved to the future than an evil heart can be transformed by its possessor moving to a different country. The real malaise behind this spiritual hysteria is not the absence of the goods advertised, or the absence of the future, but a confusion of the direction of the gaze that belongs to the dove's eyes and the direction of the gaze that belongs to the serpent's. The dove's eyes should be focused on present blessings: should see everything that is good in the present moment, should be turned with childlike hope to God who is beyond time. The serpent's eyes should be turned with prudent agnosticism to the blessings of the future. That they will take any particular form is unknown and so the soul should not be poured out on the fantasy of such a form. Instead, to the spiritual hysteric, the present is to be shunned, as the philanderer shuns the heart of the woman he has won, and looked at with the cold eyes of the serpent. To him the future alone is worthy of the eyes of the dove; but tomorrow never comes, it is always today, and his 'tender eyes grow all unkind'. His personality (like that of the person locked onto the past) begins to be taken over by that ancient serpent, Satan: the dove will never find its love-match other than in the eternal now.

The difficulties of the locked-away mind can affect the life of faith as well as the merely worldly life. It is possible for people to brood, not like Miss Havisham upon how someone has let them down, but on how they have let themselves down. A preoccupation with past failings can blind a person to the reality of present forgiveness. Openness to the present can also be vitiated by an unreasonable fixation on the future in a person's spiritual life, either in the form of a morbid fear of their fate (despair) or in the form of an unrealistic confidence (one that ignores the need for conversion) about their eternal destiny (presumption). The mind can be locked away too, even in the business of faithful love: it can be preoccupied with trying to put right what has happened in the past and is better let drop, or it can place an unreasonable confidence in the strength of the future, as in the claim, 'It'll be all right once we are married'.

The reader may be wondering by now how the theological virtue of hope is supposed to remove all these ills. The first point to be emphasized is that it is different in kind as well as in object from sublunary hope. Its object is of course qualitatively different: it looks to eternal blessedness with God, which is a different order of good from, for example, getting a new car. There are two important differences in the kind of hope it is. First, it is sure hope. Given a good will, that is deliberate co-operation with God by doing and accepting what he wants, the final outcome, blessedness, is assured in the way the plans of mice and men can never be. This means that this hope can be sustaining in the way other hope cannot be. One can hope that an operation will go well, that a book will be well received, that one will get on with someone, but this hope will not bring absolute reassurance; even the hope of a warm welcome from someone whom one knows to be faithful and loving can be dashed by that person's unexpected death. In contrast, nothing whatever outside of one's own will can damage the hope of blessedness: it is safe from any contingency. Every other disappointment, therefore, will be relative. The tribulation it brings may be a means for transmuting worldly into spiritual hope, transferring confidence from something that does not really merit it to God. For example, someone who had placed all his hope in his career may by the frustration of that hope find a space opening up in his life for the spiritual. A grain of spiritual hope may grow into a strong and vigorous plant, bringing great happiness, as a result of the uprooting of other temporal hopes that had hedged it in. In this way the tribulation of the disappointment of these hopes can be found sweet. What may be imagined by the unhoping heart to be a life of miserable disappointment may in reality be no more disappointing than the experience of listening to an adjudicator announcing the results of a competition and hearing first that one has not won the third prize, then that one hasn't won the second prize, simply to be told that one has won the first prize. The other difference between worldly and theological hope is perhaps less obvious. It is that theological hope is not in the same way future-oriented. It is, rather, eternity-oriented. This means that, from a certain aspect, it is realised hope: eternity, unlike the future, touches the present. The fatuous advertising slogan, 'The future. Now.' makes sense if it is changed to 'eternity now'. This is possible if it is thought of as an openness (for example in prayer) to the eternal God: the loss of the sense of time that people sometimes experience when they are praying confirms this. Theological hope is in some way a realised hope because it puts us in touch with God. This is true both in the sense that God's grace enables it and in the sense that in looking to God it establishes as it were a kind of rapport with him. He is not like the holiday one is hoping for next month: he is there as one hopes. This hope is both a foreshadowing and a foretaste of beatitude. Christian hope has sometimes been trivialised as though it referred simply to more time. In fact, although it does look forward to the release into a fuller existence that death gives, it also looks into it; it draws its strength from its reality as it is communicated in the present. Christian hope, although it does not see God directly, fastens onto him, and unlike worldly hope which endangers vitality on the rocks of uncertainty, from this fastening draws a depth of life elsewhere unavailable. The desire for this or that in the future becomes the desire for God: perfected, this desire is eternal life.

We have looked at the way theological hope is superior to the hope that relates to a temporal future. It can take away from the latter the consuming quality that imprisons the soul and offer a much deeper satisfaction. It is perhaps less obvious how it has a similar transforming effect on the tendency of the mind to become locked into the past with regret or nostalgia. This becomes clearer if we remember that theological hope does not reach out to the future so much as to eternity. Its proper point of reference is what is outside time. It is therefore in some sense the equivalent on a supernatural level of the natural faculty of memory. Memory is a kind of symbol or evidence of the eternal. It bears witness that there is in the past, recaptured by the memory, another dimension than that of pure temporality. Being made present, the past is given an eternal aspect. Memory leads us to hope for the end of all absence. It reminds us, prophetically, of the hope of eternal presence: it reminds us of God. Christian hope is the realisation of this presence, albeit through a glass darkly. It can fill, as it were, that part of the mind that is not satisfied with the business of the present insofar as it relates to the time and space of the creation. Instead of this part of the mind (or faculty of the soul) locking itself away into the past (or the future) it can lock onto eternity: this, unlike the husks of time, is vivifying. This idea may be more easily grasped if we consider the implications of the word 'recollection'. It can mean both remembering and being in a state of prayerful awareness of God. And 'recollection' in the spiritual sense is a sort of remembering of who we are. In his interpretation of the parable of the Prodigal Son, St Augustine describes the far country that the son goes to as 'forgetfulness of God'[9] – returning to him is remembering him, recollection, hope. To remember in this way is to animadvert to our source, our beginning, to the fact that, as Wordsworth puts it,

> Not in entire forgetfulness,
> And not in utter nakedness,
> But trailing clouds of glory do we come
> From God who is our home.[10]

The next chapter will consider more closely how theological hope is vivifying, how it liberates us from our cage of time and space. It will also look more fully at how this hope can grow in tribulation, so that the tribulation is sweet.

CHAPTER EIGHT

REMEMBERING ZION

*To remember God with hope is to live
in the dawn of eternal life*

Christian hope remembers God. This supernatural kind of
hope does not simply absorb the human faculty for looking
forward, it also absorbs the faculty of memory. It replaces
both the backward and the forward looking activity of the
locked-away mind, insofar as these activities arise from misplaced aspiration rather than reasonable prudence. Its
remembering is a reaching out not to the past, but to the
eternal. This chapter considers this reaching out: how, like
faith, it gives us power to come close to others in love; how it
is sown and strengthened in prayer, and how it can use
tribulation to become more purely focused on the one source
of true life.

The value of this way of using the faculty of memory is
expressed in T.S. Eliot's *Four Quartets*:

> This is the use of memory:
> For liberation – not less of love but expanding
> Of love beyond desire, and so liberation
> From the future as well as the past.[1]

The heart, which is capable of embracing far more than is
offered by any particular location in time and space, looks for
its fulfilment neither as it were backwards to the past nor
forwards to the future, but upwards to the eternity of God.
The desire that is transcended here is the desire (whether
nostalgia or longing) for any particular good: nothing less
than God is allowed to be ultimately important. This brings
'liberation' and 'expanding of love' because the freeing of the
heart from being dominated by any particular aspiration
leaves an emptiness that God himself can fill. In God nothing
is neglected – everything lives and moves and has its being in
God and God dwells in everything – therefore the person
who is filled with God is able to include everything in his

love. Not only can he love everyone (not just those he finds gratifying and those only when he finds them gratifying), but he loves what is best in them. Even the stony-hearted have God dwelling deep within them, though they may have cut themselves off from his light and strength, and this love can reach out to God within them and help them to allow God's love to dissolve the hard shell that comes between them and him. One might say that this love loves the stony-hearted better than they love themselves. It also reaches people on a deeper level than a love whose motive is the pleasure taken in their qualities, whether these be beauty and intelligence or nobility of character and spiritual insight. It therefore offers an escape from that loneliness that can co-exist with the brushing and entanglement of personalities (or bodies): it is an escape from loneliness and an achievement of communion not only for the person who is loving, but also for the person who is loved. The person who loves like this goes about destroying loneliness, evoking a love in others that enables them to melt the loneliness of yet others. With a love like this one can never be lonely: those one loves may choose to be, but they have every encouragement not to be. The ending of loneliness is possible because people meet, not on the level where particular backgrounds, interests, likes and aversions separate them, but in God, the one God in whom all find themselves and find themselves one.

This is what it is to hope in God. It brings not only communion, but peace and joy: peace because there is nothing to worry about either in the past or in the future, and joy because this hope is a knowledge that if we do our part, God will give us eternal beatitude – himself. This is why St Paul writes to the Romans:

May the God of hope fill you with all joy and peace in believing so that by the power of the Holy Spirit you may abound in hope.[2]

The communion, peace and joy are a foretaste and indistinct participation in heaven. This is the communion of the saints:

communion, not yet perfectly realised, with other pilgrims to the heavenly city and with those there. This is the peace that passes understanding because it does not depend on knowing the details of how everything has been part of God's providence or on grasping with the mind how everything is going to be all right, but issues from hope in God who is so much greater than anything the mind can comprehend. This is the joy which Jesus promises that no-one will take from us, a joy so God-centred and free from selfish clinging that in this joy we live, in Blake's words, 'in eternity's sunrise'.[3] This hope enables us to live in some sense out of time, or better, freed from time.

The means to this hope is to remember who we are, from whom we come and to whom we are going. The story of the king's son enacts this truth. It tells of how a royal prince went to a far and foreign country and there gradually fell into a mean, ignoble and contemptible life. There he forgot who he was. He had only to remember and all the richness, nobility and glory of his father's kingdom was available to him for the asking. We are heirs to the kingdom of heaven: we have only to remember that we are. In Christian tradition this kingdom is symbolically called the heavenly Jerusalem, or Zion. This gives a special meaning to the following psalm:

> By the rivers of Babylon
> there we sat and wept,
> remembering Zion;
> on the poplars that grew there
> we hung up our harps.
>
> For it was there that they asked us,
> our captors, for songs,
> our oppressors, for joy.
> 'Sing to us', they said,
> 'One of Zion's songs.'
>
> O how could we sing
> the song of the Lord
> on alien soil?

If I forget you, Jerusalem,
let my right hand wither![4]

The absence of joy here is simply the shadow of true joy: it is the refusal to squander the heart on anything incomplete and partial that will block its hopeful gaze to God. Music, the perfect harmony of perfect love, is reserved for heaven. This absolute devotion cannot be given to our captors and oppressors, those things that would take us from God by making themselves idols so our hope was rooted not where it can never be betrayed, but where it will be disappointed, in time. Here, in time, we are exiles from our true kingdom. To remember that kingdom is so important that to forget it would be a greater loss than the loss of a right hand, the loss of our chief means of manipulating things in this world. No influence on this world, no amount of technology can replace this memory if it is lost, this most precious hope.

To lose it is to be in the position of those described in Plato's story of the cave.[5] Shackled in a position where they can only see shadows, they are ignorant of the world of daylight with a ferocity that would put to death one who would tell them about it. The daylight is to their shadows what eternity is to the limitations of a life lived with the heart set exclusively on the things of this world. How then is the heart to be set on the eternal, how are we to remember Zion? By prayer. This can take many forms. It can be the receiving of the Eternal Word made flesh in holy communion. Here faith knows that which is unseen and never passes away in the consecrated bread and wine and hope sets the heart on it; here the life beyond time is received. Prayer can be the saying of words, silently or aloud, drawing the mind and heart to intentions articulated by sacred tradition. It can be the repetition of a simple phrase or word ('Jesus' for example) that takes the mind and stills it in a good stillness so that the soul can be open to holiness. It can be the silence beyond all of these that simply rests in God.

Above all, prayer is desire. It is not the same desire that T.S. Eliot talks of transcending, because it is not the desire for anything in particular. Little desires of this kind have been sold like so many little pearls for the purchase of this one great desire, the pearl of great price.[6] This seeks not to subordinate God to one's own purposes but rather to subordinate one's own purposes to him, to raise the heart and mind to him. In choosing God it chooses everything: it gives up absolute preference for any aspect of creation in favour of a preference for the absolute, the Creator who is at the source of everything. If the Creator is known, everything is known from the inside, as it were. If the kingdom of heaven is sought first, then all other things are given to the seeker.[7] The life of prayer is the purification of this desire. Desire breeds hope: this hope puts us in a sort of touch with the source of all joy and peace; this leads to a deeper desire which engenders a stronger hope and so on in a virtuous circle which sears the life of God ever deeper in our soul. This process is one of purification because as the hope and desire deepen, so they have less and less to do with the benefits that spring from communion with God and more and more to do with God himself. For example, to begin with, prayer may bring with it warm and comfortable feelings. As it progresses it may be more a matter of facing humbly the hardness and coldness in ourselves that distance God from us, something which, on the surface, it is less painful not to do. To go on with it requires a purer desire and hope than that which was needed at the start, since any admixture of desire or hope for comfort and warmth will be disappointed. So desire and hope are purified and tend more and more to want God just for himself, and less and less for his consolations. There is a parallel process with the life of virtue. At first there may be the happiness of achievement, which for all the good in it contains a great deal of self-satisfaction, but as the conscience becomes more sensitive it becomes more and more aware that, in the words of the prophet Isaiah, 'All our righteousnesses are as filthy rags',[8] more and more aware of our desolation short of union with God.

The actual practice of prayer, of the hopeful life, requires times when one is alone and silent. In this silence one seeks to enter one's own heart and dwell on the desire in it, the desire for God – the one love which is guaranteed to be reciprocated. This desire calls to God and grows into a hope, not of the worldly 'it would be nice if' kind, but a hope that is a kind of knowledge, an assurance that can become a strong and diamond stillness: the presence of God. In this mental prayer there can be words inwardly articulated that speak the love and the hope, or there may only be words repeated that keep the mind happy while something more important is going on. Or there may simply be silence, the silence of desires for this or that particular thing forgotten, the silence of the stilling of superficial activity, the silence of wordless aspiration. If this practice is kept up – with the best possible disposition and circumstances it would require a minimum of twenty minutes a day – then in time other aspects of one's life will begin to grow out of prayer. What it is good and fitting to do will come to mind with natural ease and supernatural light. Things that happen will more easily be seen in proportion: it won't be that they cease to hurt sometimes – prayer is not an anaesthetic – but, in the awareness of a meaning and a love at the deep root of everything, there will be a sense of a greater harmony of which even the greatest dereliction cannot be the last note.

To pray is to live in the present as acutely as is possible because it is to reach into the eternal source of the present reality. This accounts for the loss of the sense of time that can happen in prayer, mentioned in the last chapter. In prayer one lives, as spontaneously as a child, a life undarkened by the shadow of the past or the future. There is an important difference, however, between the image (natural childhood) and the reality (supernatural prayer). The latter is the conscious direction taken by free and mature decision. It is therefore able to guard itself from corruption. This is not to say that the childhood spontaneity is necessarily going to be corrupted, but that only by conscious choice of God is it going to achieve a stability of innocence. In an age which has lost the sense of the supernatural, there is a tendency to over-exalt youth because it is the nearest thing that can be seen to sanctity, whose natural image it is. Children, and their birth-days and so on, can even be seen as virtually sacred. Real sanctity, however, is a kind of supernatural childhood which is acquired by a process of deliberate opening to God, deliberate choice of the eternal present. The children of God, whether they have reacquired their childhood or transformed it, have supernaturally what children have naturally – the fullness of the eternal present; but they have the wisdom to be able to keep it.

The value of Christian hope has been emphasized. It may be less clear how it can flourish in tribulation or give a person the power to find tribulation sweet. It may be observed that troubles can diminish hope; that a person with a confident, positive attitude to life may, through their affliction, be lured into the slough of despond. It is no part of the argument of this book that suffering inevitably produces an increase of the virtues of faith, hope and love. It is rather maintained that, for the possessor of a determinedly positive attitude to it, suffer-ing can be the occasion of such a flourishing in the life of the soul that its bitterness is secondary to this life's sweetness. A metaphor that captures both the reaction of the person to whom trouble brings a despairing attitude and that of the person to whom it brings an increase of hope is that of a fire. A feeble fire is extinguished by a gust of wind; one that has really got under way burns more vigorously under its influ-ence. The metaphor also serves to illustrate the life of the soul in the process of growth. When the flame is kindled it may at first be able to take gentle gusts, although not fierce ones, but as it grows so will it be able to benefit from increasingly strong wind. The metaphor of the fire also expresses in another way what happens in the life of the soul: the pieces of wood on it can be envisaged as so many crosses. At first the fire will only take little crosses – heavy lumps of wood are likely to put it out – but as it grows so it will take bigger and bigger crosses: where once it would have been extinguished, it will burn more fiercely.

Hope can go on burning more brightly through the increase of troubles because the hope is being placed more and more exclusively where it cannot be disappointed. One could say that it is becoming less and less misplaced, or that it is becoming more and more pure. One way of looking at the process is to imagine a very special hotel where the higher one goes in the level of management the more reliable and competent the people who work there. One hopes that the waiter will provide the service one wants; one is disappointed. Instead of giving up, one places one's hope in the head waiter. When this too is disappointed, one doesn't despair but asks to see the chef. Perhaps he can see that things are all right for a while, but when he proves unreliable one turns to the manager of the hotel. One's last hope turns out to be one's best hope: the manager shows an intelligence, a trustworthiness and a competence that were beyond any of his staff. So it is with the virtue of hope. At first, for example, one might place one's hope in one's youthful good looks and charm as a means to happiness. Age could then take away the good looks and illness could produce an irritability that vitiated the charm. One might then hope in one's achievement. Circumstances might thwart this and so on. The end of the road – the place where hope can be placed without being disappointed – is God; it is not personal achievement of any kind, even the greatest virtue. St Thérèse wrote of appearing before God at the evening of her life with empty hands:[9] she would not place her hope even in the greatest of personal goods, her own virtue. The Scylla and Charybdis that beset the voyager to perfect hope in God are despair and presumption. There can be despair of there being anything to hope for, because the haven where one's hope rested on its way to something worthier turned out to offer no real comfort. There can be presumption that there is no need to hope in God, because what one has placed one's hope in (one's own moral achievements, for example) appears to offer enough.

Tribulation can be the occasion of the fire of hope burning more brightly because it tends to close off lesser hopes, making greater room for the great hope, hope in God. This does not mean that tribulation is necessary for a pure hope in God: however, fallen human nature is such that there is a tendency (rather than a necessity) to set one's hopes too low – to use the hotel image, there is a tendency to rely on one of the waiters, rather than on the manager. Even something that is at first not hoped in at all can seduce hope. For example, a person may be of exemplary modesty, not expecting any praise, but by dint of receiving it gradually come to rely upon it for their own sense of worth. They may then experience the tribulation of losing their good reputation, not through their own fault but because of a misunderstanding. At this point they may (to give the two extreme possibilities) either react with bitterness or use the tribulation as a caustic agent to scour from their soul the improper placing of their hope in the praise they receive from others. If they do the latter they are free to place it where it properly belongs, in God, who alone gives a person an unassailable value. Various tribulations can be used in this way to purify the soul from placing reliance (or hope) in the various comforts that those tribulations deny, and so to free it to place its hope in God. The stronger the hope in God in the first place, the greater the tribulation it can make use of for its greater strengthening. An analogy is the use of weights for training: the stronger the muscles in the first place, the greater the weights that can be used for their strengthening.

It may be objected that this will work for detaching one from various indulgences, but that there is a suffering so intense that it seems to assail not any particular comfort but the very spirit of life itself. How can this purify hope? Obviously at this point the soul is playing for very high stakes: it is not a matter of improving in this or that respect, but a battle between the most heroic hope and despair. In this sort of suffering hope is being purified of any sort of reliance in time at all: it must rest in the eternal God, or nowhere. We come back to the locked-away mind. In the examples we examined in the last chapter the mind was locked away to an extreme extent: the soul was almost lost in the past or the future. A healthy soul is in nothing like this state, but that does not mean that it is as focused in the present as is desirable: except in ecstasy or deep prayer, it is likely to be distracted or dispersed to some extent. Intense suffering can cast such a shadow over both past and future as to make this virtually impossible. There is no comfort to be had from the past, no afterglow remains from it to light up the present; the future cannot be coped with at all – the troubles of the moment are such that even to imagine such another moment (still less the morrow) is to overburden the soul impossibly. It is only possible to live in the merest instant, being absolutely dependent on the strength of God alone. To do so is to be strong with the only strength that will survive everything and truly to be liberated 'from the future as well as the past'.

CHAPTER NINE

LOVE AND THE GREY COAT

Loving God joyfully

We have considered how faith and hope may grow in tribulation; how they may be seen as so valuable that the suffering takes a secondary place, like so much Christmas wrapping paper on the floor – not wanted for itself, but the outward covering of something joyfully received. Even so, it may be thought, does this amount to paradise on earth? To explain this degree of joy we need to consider as well the third and the greatest of the theological virtues, love. Faith and hope relate to our life on earth: love is the specifically paradisal virtue. In heaven, faith is replaced with knowledge, hope with possession; love, however, is a child of both heaven and earth. It alone can transform earth into paradise. Love never ends: where love is, God is, and God is eternal. Love brings God, brings heaven to earth.

However, on earth, this supernatural love needs the other virtues to serve, as it were, as its feeding tubes linked to heaven, transmitting the celestial nourishment that it needs to stay alive on earth. Faith is a gift from God by which we know him and his love for us. Hope is the gift from him by which we reach out to him and his love with confidence. Because of the faith and hope that we have in God, we are able to return his love. The love we give him is also his gift to us. This chapter will discuss this gift and how, like faith and hope, it can grow in tribulation.

By way of analogy, an example of human love can serve as a starting-point for our discussion of the love of God. In Shakespeare's *The Winter's Tale* Florizel addresses his beloved Perdita as follows:

> What you do
> Still betters what is done. When you speak, sweet,
> I'ld have you do it ever; when you sing,
> I'ld have you buy and sell so; so give alms;
> Pray so; and for the ord'ring your affairs,

To sing them too. When you do dance, I wish you
A wave o' th' sea, that you might ever do
Nothing but that; move still, still so,
And own no other function. Each your doing
(So singular in each particular)
Crowns what you are doing in the present deeds,
That all your acts are queens.[1]

What is remarkable here is how happy Florizel is with everything Perdita does. This is eloquently summed up in his telling her 'All your acts are queens'. Whatever she does appears to him perfection. The distinguishing mark of his love is joy: joy in all she does. Florizel does not find joy in her actions as a detached observer of artistic excellence, but because they are *hers* and he loves her. Love like this takes joy in any expression of the beloved. In the same way, love of God takes joy in anything that his providence ordains. The Lord of the dance delights his lover as Perdita does hers. The sea symbolizes the eternal depths from which his actions come. The wave, where the opposites of activity and repose are transcended, as the apparent oxymoron 'move still' suggests, is an apt symbol of his creative immutability. His calm and infinite goodness 'still betters what is done'. Of course, Florizel is not talking about God, but any love – especially when expressed by a great poet – is an obscure recognition of divinity.

The greater the love of God, the less the lover's joy is dependent on pleasure or the absence of pain, because it is joy in him, not in benefits to be had from him. St Thérèse in her great love for God found joy like this in him at the darkest time, saying,

> I always see the good side of things. There are those who take everything in the way to cause themselves the most trouble. For me, it's the opposite. If I have nothing but pure suffering, if the sky is so dark that I can see no break in the clouds, well, I make it my joy![2]

For St Thérèse whatever happens comes from God's loving

hands and so, because she loves him, she is able to find joy in it, however bleak it is in appearance. 'The good side of things' she refers to can be seen as God's presence in the heart of his creation. This is a reason for joy even in darkness. She gives an example of darkness (the specific troubles which will be considered in Chapter Eleven) and comments, 'They make me more glorious than a queen'.[3] This is a striking echo of St John's presentation of the passion of Jesus as an entering into his kingly glory.[4]

Love finds joy in the presence of the beloved and also in doing things for the beloved. In Shakespeare's *The Tempest* Prospero, Miranda's father, makes Ferdinand carry logs to try his love for her. This is not something a prince, as he is, would normally do, but, he reflects,

> some kinds of baseness
> Are nobly undergone; and most poor matters
> Point to rich ends. This my mean task
> Would be as heavy to me as odious, but
> The mistress which I serve quickens what's dead,
> And makes my labours pleasures.[5]

'Most poor matters point to rich ends' and just as Ferdinand is willing to undertake a 'mean task' for Miranda, so love of God, in the words of George Herbert, 'makes drudgery divine'. The humble task performed for God is a pane of glass through which heaven is seen:

> Nothing can be so mean
> Which with his tincture (for thy sake)
> Will not grow bright and clean.[6]

Ferdinand's actions, however, are a preparation for a state where he can wonder at Miranda in the way Florizel admires Perdita. So with the love of God, the one thing needful is not primarily love's labour but contemplation of his perfection.[7] Heaven is seen through the humble tasks, but they are not heaven themselves. This is present in germ in the love that motivates them. The love, in itself, has surpassing value. A social milieu where greater value is given to activity directed to the future than to contemplation may have obscured this truth, but it is implied in St Paul's justly celebrated definition of love. This does not even mention activity explicitly – its emphasis is on acceptance and enjoyment:

> Love is patient and kind; love is not jealous or boastful; it is not arrogant or rude. Love does not insist on its own way; it is not irritable or resentful; it does not rejoice at wrong, but rejoices in the right. Love bears all things, believes all things, hopes all things, endures all things.[8]

Loving actions are implied in love being kind and 'love bears all things' can be seen as including bearing the burden of activity. Otherwise, love is said to show itself principally in the absence of negative reactions. If we think about the sort of people that it is pleasant to live with (rather than about the heroic acts of love that we would like to glory in ourselves undertaking) then this emphasis makes sense. The preferred shipboard companion of Chapter Four clearly falls under this definition. Much of love in practice is tolerance. Christian love is patient: it accepts the harshness of others, not as something to be avenged, but as a mountain stream takes heated metal thrust into it – the heat is insignificant to its freshness and coolness. This of course is only possible for one living the life of the holy tree whose 'hidden root has planted quiet in the night'. It avoids the assertiveness of a life that looks to 'the glass of outer weariness' for its sense of identity: such a life needs to run down the achievements of others and assert its own. Because its meaning is not within, but staked out in the instability of time and space, it must insist on its own way and take issue when it is interfered with. Only a love rooted in that joy where 'the holy branches start, and all the trembling flowers they bear' can rejoice in the right irrespective of where it is found, whether or not it reinforces an egoistic sense of worth.

Perhaps the most challenging thing about St Paul's definition of love when it is contrasted with romantic notions is the emphasis on simply taking what comes. Dostoevsky catches this contrast:

> Love in action is a harsh and dreadful thing compared with love in dreams. Love in dreams is greedy for immediate action, rapidly performed and in the sight of all. Men will even give their lives if only the ordeal does not last long and is soon over, with all onlooking and applauding as though on the stage. But active love is labour and fortitude ...[9]

This labour and this fortitude is bearing all things and enduring all things with the strength of absolute faith and absolute hope. It means, for example, accepting harsh words without bitterness not seven times but seventy times seven; it means allowing people to be themselves, even when those selves seem to crush our very life (an appearance only, because it is the ego-life and not the true life that is being crushed); it means a benignity that encompasses everyone without exception, like the sun that God makes to shine on the just and the unjust.[10] The rightness of St Paul's definition becomes clear if we contrast with it the romantic notion, as described by Dostoevsky, from the point of view of the recipient of the love. It is not dissimilar to life with the two shipboard companions. Life with the person who romanticises his achievements in love (not necessarily romantic love) is an endless attempt either to appear impressed and notice the supposedly strikingly generous attention and consideration one is being given, or to put up with or attempt to assuage the sulkiness and withdrawn moodiness that comes from not showing that one notices.

The love that is labour and fortitude creates a very different atmosphere for its recipient: to enjoy it is like basking in the sun that God makes to shine on the just and the unjust alike. One never feels rushed or pressured or oppressed by one's lack of ability: this love is patient. One never has the uncomfortable feeling that only the other person is right – they realise that theirs is not the only way of doing things. One is never afraid of irritating them or anxious about not being forgiven. One knows that one's joy in any good achieved will be shared. Above all, one knows that one will be endlessly tolerated and unconditionally accepted. The effect of all this is that one is free to be oneself in the best possible way. Mother Teresa of Calcutta was speaking once to a large audience. Afterwards she made a point of thanking one of them. This person was puzzled by her thanks. She was told that she had looked at Mother Teresa with love in her eyes and this had made the ordeal of speaking easy and free of anxiety – her words were simply addressed to this person. Someone who loves us in the Pauline sense listens to who we are, gives us the peace and confidence to be that person. It is a common enough experience that some people are easier to talk to than others: they seem to give one freedom and even intelligence by the quality of their attention. The truly loving person allows us to unfold and blossom: we may not even be aware that they are giving us this until they are taken away from us. The cost to them is the foregoing of any indulgence of the impulse to fashion us according to their own pattern when that conflicts with ours and the patient bearing of any pain that the way we are brings them. The reward to them is to see us blossom and to enjoy a life enriched by a personality that looks at the world in a different way from their own and therefore adds to it.

These reflections about what it means to love people bear directly on the love of God. Jesus said that what is done to the least of his brethren is done to him.[11] Furthermore, this is how God is to be loved in a more direct way. There is a sense in which we can allow God himself to unfold and blossom. The cost and the reward are analogous, though greater. We pay by foregoing the desire to fashion our life and the world according to our own impulses and by patiently bearing the pain given us by God's purposes for us and the way the world is. The reward is seeing God blossom: that is, seeing good in everything. Here it is not just a matter of enjoying a life enriched by a personality that looks at the world in a different way: it is a matter of enjoying a life made rich by seeing the world from the point of view of its Creator, filled, that is, with its very meaning.

What, however, has bearing pain got to do with the joy that

we have said belongs to love? Here we come to the central point of this chapter, and indeed of this book. It has been hinted at in the analogies given in Chapter Two, of a knight willingly bearing pain to prove his love for his lady and of someone happily taking trouble on another's behalf, and in Ferdinand bearing his logs. Meister Eckhart, the medieval mystic, expresses it by asking us to imagine that there is a man whom we particularly wish to please. If we know that he likes us best in a grey coat, will we not be happy to wear a grey coat?[12] For the lover of God, the stripy tunic of pleasure may be less attractive than the grey coat of suffering, when that is the clothing that his blessed purposes come in.

A grey coat is an apt image for suffering: it recalls the whole twilight world, caught between life and death, imagined by Beckett. It evokes the colourlessness of a life drained by suffering, its seeming lack of possibility and the lack of impact it makes on others. It is redolent of the suffering servant, described by Isaiah:

> He had no form or comeliness that we should look at him, and no beauty that we should desire him. He was despised and rejected by men; a man of sorrows, and acquainted with grief; and as one from whom men hide their faces; he was despised, and we esteemed him not.[13]

At the same time the fact that it is a coat identifies it as belonging to that which is exterior. To the outward eye it is to be shunned, but inside of it may be something very different. What makes this possible is love. It is necessarily a pure love, which delights to give. It has its echo in the trouble which a tired mother will take to prepare a meal for her children. It may cost her a lot of effort, but it will be more rewarding, more joyful, even, because of her love. The joy in this case is not in the fatigue or in the fraying of nerves; it is in the being able to give. That these children should be sustained by her is very dear to her heart; the trouble that it causes her is a secondary consideration. So it is with the love of God. Suffering, whether it be fatigue and fraying of nerves or something more terrible, is never in itself something in which to take joy. It isn't desirable that it should be more of a focus of attention than can be helped – St Thérèse felt that it showed a lack of delicacy towards God to animadvert to it, since that aspect of what was going on was so far from his intention for her. Rather the joy is in being able to give full-hearted co-operation to God and in being able to receive his love. This exchange of love depends on faith that God does want co-operation in a plan that does exist, despite the subjectively unrewarding nature of what is going on, and faith that even as it is unfolding one is the object of his particular love. It is also supported by the hope of this love, both that received and that given, being known more fully.

The joy is taken in the giving and receiving of love; in the relationship. If the suffering is not exactly 'a lover's pinch, which hurts, and is desir'd' (as Shakespeare's Cleopatra says of her death)[14] nonetheless it is the acceptable shadow of something most dear, a giving and receiving of love with the Lover at the heart of creation. One is, as it were, in on the secret. It doesn't mean what it seems to on the face of it. Despite the grey coat that covers them, in the words of Hopkins,

There lives the dearest freshness deep down things.[15]

The joy is secret, hidden, shared. There is a mutual loving purpose that, if it does not make it nugatory, takes suffering away from the centre of relevance. The pain tends towards that of one giving birth. Faith knows that a love-child is being born, and joy in this pushes the suffering towards the periphery of what is happening. In the happiness of the birth, the celebration of love, the pain is outside of where the real life is, outside the soul; inside the soul is God himself and being there he is a sort of shield from it. The innermost being rejoices in his glorious purposes and is in some measure detached from the outer weariness where the ego-life is tormented. It is as though a man were with his family who are most dear to him, all safe within his house, unworried by the wind blowing down the michaelmas daisies in the garden outside. When the opportunity comes he'll prop them up again, but their fall won't stop him being happy with his beloved family. Another way of looking at it is to say that the loving sufferer already enjoys in an obscure mode the life of heaven, transcending space and time, and so the pains of this world, for all their hurt, don't tear at his heart of hearts, where his heavenly treasure is.[16] That doesn't mean that emotionally and physically all is calm, but he is aware of a deeper life where there is peace. In this life he is being given something that gives joy on a different plane to that on which the suffering affects him. Imagine that, through no fault of your own, you have a doorbell that makes an unpleasant, grating noise: someone you dearly love and have long expected is coming. He has a special way of announcing his arrival – three long rings. Suddenly your aesthetic sensibilities are savaged, your ears are assaulted thrice by a horrible noise. How horrible is it, *really*? Perhaps St Thérèse was reacting in similar way to her agonizing suffering when she said 'Oh, don't you worry about me, I have come to the point of not being able to suffer any more, because all suffering is sweet to me'.[17]

A vigorous hope can be purified in suffering. The same sort of pattern applies to its sister virtue, love. When one person asks another person, 'Do you only love me for my body?' they don't necessarily mean they would prefer not to be found attractive or that they wish to withhold physical affection, but that their person is more than their body and that they wish to be valued in their wholeness. This is the sort of love that makes marriage possible, in sickness and in health. A love that depends entirely on bodily attractiveness is not going to be good enough to bring happiness in marriage. In the same way a love of God – a delighted rejoicing in his purposes – that is limited to being content when the good things of creation are organised for our pleasure is not good enough to give us happiness here or hereafter. We need a truer, deeper love that takes him, not according to our pleasure, but as he comes. That love is our own greatest possible good, so if tribulation weans us off the milk of being limited by our own pleasure, then it does us a service and, if we take it in the spirit that allows us to be done this service, there is no reason why we should not find it sweet. This is why it is said, 'The Lord disciplines him whom he loves'; why St James says, 'Count it all joy, my brethren when you meet various trials'; why St Peter says, 'You rejoice, though now for a little while you may have to suffer various trials'.[18] These trials can be seen as a kind of training in the highest love, a process of changing the wilfulness that would confine us to what we are capable of imagining as good for us. They give us the possibility of transforming our will so that it becomes one with God's, a state in which it wills and thus reaches everything that is good for us – in any other state, only a lesser good is possible. St Thérèse had reached that state when she attributed her gaiety to the fact that God showed her that the only joy on earth is to accomplish his will.

As the will is progressively transformed in this way, so the heart of suffering is gradually removed, whatever afflictions it imposes outwardly. We begin to relax our determination to have what we have decided we want in the face of reality that says it must be otherwise. We flow with the tide of the creation, we are one with its purposes; our will is the same as its Creator's, we no longer experience the single jarring note of our limited ego-life, but the total harmony that is known from within the life of God. Tribulation is seen as sowing for a harvest:

> Those who are sowing in tears
> will sing when they reap.
> They go out, they go out, full of tears,
> carrying seed for the sowing:
> they come back, they come back, full of song,
> carrying their sheaves.[19]

To the soul in loving communion with God that has begun its life in eternity on earth, those sheaves are in the sowing.

CHAPTER TEN

RIPENESS IS ALL

Love blossoming in desolation

In the last chapter we considered how love, like hope, can grow in suffering. This chapter will develop and illustrate this discussion. With the help of insights from literature it will look at how love can blossom in desolation.

To love is to be supernaturally strong, sharing in the power of God who is love. Blake, a visionary poet, had the intuition of how this supernatural power could enter through suffering:

> For a tear is an intellectual thing;
> And a sigh is the sword of an angel king,
> And the groan of a martyr's woe
> Is an arrow from the Almighty's bow![1]

The connotation of the word 'intellectual' is that of belonging to the spiritual realm, beyond the mutability of passing emotion. The power (symbolized in the poem by the sword and the arrow) can be seen as entering, as it were, into the space created by the suffering. Seeing it this way is another way of understanding the process of the purification of love. Desire is centred on something that is less than absolute good (less than God) and that desire is thwarted by suffering, which can be seen as a sort of bereavement when it takes away something which had been a joy and comfort, or as a disappointment when it takes away something hoped for. In either case there is the pain of absence, emptiness. However, this very emptiness (given the right disposition: an openness to God) is a space in which God can dwell. The heart, suffering because of its attachment to a partial good of which it is now deprived, is free to embrace its absolute good which is God, as expressed in his will for this particular moment. This is not to say that the suffering is abolished, but the heart is taken out of it and taken into God. The taking of the heart into God is the greatest possible good. It is not necessarily impossible without suffering, but it is not so easy. In the absence of suffering there is the tendency to love created things unrealistically, to love them instead of God (that is, superficially) rather than to love them in him. If the heart is fixed on God then nothing else can have an absolute importance or be an absolute pain. Everything, however, can be loved in the best possible way, as God loves it. The process of the purification of love, then, is one of emptying of selfishness, of superficiality, of 'outer weariness'.

This will be illustrated by an examination of Shakespeare's tragedy *King Lear*, a play which shows how apparent disintegration and painful emptying can lead to something of the life of God growing within the person. Although the play is of course a product of a Christian culture, the process is not presented in explicitly Christian terminology. This is an indication of the universality of the reality that the Christian terms describe. It may seem odd that a book called *Paradise on Earth* should be focusing on what has often been held to be Shakespeare's bleakest tragedy. Yet, of course, this paradise of which à Kempis and the saints speak is not a paradise brought about by having everything turn out in a pleasing way. It is rather a transformation of attitude: the kingdom of heaven is within you.[2] And tragic art is about facing and accepting the dark side of human existence, particularly death:

> Men must endure
> Their going hence even as their coming hither,
> Ripeness is all.[3]

The ripeness is the mature soul, the transformed attitude that will say with Job: 'The Lord gave, and the Lord has taken away; blessed be the name of the Lord'.[4] And in that soul, which lives for ever, is real good, the glory that is to come with which St Paul thought the sufferings of the present not worth comparing.[5] That glory, as we have tried to show, is not simply reserved for the future, but is present during the sufferings of this life, even when it is not felt. It is this that matters – not passing pleasures.

Given that this is the case, it is not surprising that tragedy has been seen as embodying the highest of human values. It is concerned with the nobility of the human soul. There is a kind of exaltation in seeing what the soul can face, well understood by Yeats in his poem, *Lapis Lazuli*:

> Hamlet and Lear are gay;
> Gaiety transfiguring all that dread.
> All men have aimed at, found and lost;
> Black out; Heaven blazing into the head:
> Tragedy wrought to its uttermost.[6]

In the black – the darkness of our exile – is 'Heaven blazing into the head', paradise on earth. It is worth looking at secular literature, as well as explicitly religious writing, to see the universality of this law of human possibility. It is not something confined to religious vocabulary and practices, but a transformation yearned for in the very substance of the human spirit. It is not therefore surprising that our greatest poet and playwright, who saw life steadily and saw it whole, should be able to help our understanding of it.

At the start of the play, King Lear announces his intention to give up ruling, with its burdens, and his land. This is not a real self-emptying, however (though in the end it becomes that), because he offers his authority and territory in exchange for the declared love of his daughters. He would possess love and, after the manner not recommended by Blake's poem,[7] bind it to himself. That invites a false love, which two of his daughters offer. The third daughter, Cordelia, really does love him and finds herself perplexed, not wishing to be involved in the hypocritical show of her sisters:

What shall Cordelia speak? Love, and be silent.[8]

The silence in which her love is to be received echoes the silence in which God's love is to be received. Its reception requires a faith that will not depend on signs, but will see, in the 'nothing'[9] that Cordelia speaks in response to attempted manipulation, a love that is the truer for not yielding to it. For Lear, however, at this point love is a possession to be traded. He rejects Cordelia. He asks one of her suitors how much he requires as a dowry if he is to cease his 'quest of love'.[10] Because he has not had the response he wanted from her he withdraws his offer of a dowry, saying, 'Her price is fallen'.[11] The first suitor refuses her on these terms, but the second has an altogether different view of love:

> Love's not love
> When it is mingled with regards that stands
> Aloof from th' entire point.[12]

For him, it has nothing to do with trading or possessing. In contrast to Cordelia's other suitor, he offers her a pure love. Cordelia, without her dowry, is 'most rich being poor'[13] – rich inwardly, poor outwardly. Lear from now on journeys towards this understanding of the first beatitude, 'Blessed are the poor in spirit, for theirs is the kingdom of heaven'.[14]

His first painful understanding is of the falseness of the seeming riches offered him by his other two daughters. He has an attendant Fool who underscores the poorness of the deal he has made. He finds he is not given the attention he was used to as king and asks, 'Who is it that can tell me who I am?' and is told, 'Lear's shadow'.[15] That is, on the level of identity given by the satisfaction of predilections and aversions (such as not liking yoghurt) he is fading away. On another level, however, room is being created for a silent shipboard companion, as it were. Before he can trust the silence (Cordelia is silent; God, who is love, is beyond words), he has to learn the wrongness of his trust in the outward shows of his false daughters. The first is unwelcoming: he transfers his trust to the other, who, he says, 'I am sure is kind'.[16] An awareness is beginning to dawn, however, about his treatment of Cordelia: 'I did her wrong'.[17]

The second false daughter is also unwelcoming. He becomes involved in an argument about how many attendant knights he is to be allowed. The first daughter had asked him to reduce the number: the second now asks him to bring no more than twenty-five. He turns back to the first, who is visiting her sister, and says:

> I'll go with thee,
> Thy fifty yet doth double five-and-twenty
> And thou art twice her love.[18]

She asks

> What need you five and twenty? ten? or five?[19]

Her sister adds

> What need one?[20]

In rage he goes out into a storm. The sisters agree that they will only receive him alone in their houses. His comment on the number of attendants he can have shows what he is to learn: for him love is to be numbered – fifty is twice twenty-five, so twice the love. In reality, however, love (God is love) is infinite, not to be confused with the contingencies of its terrestrial expression.

By linking it to the number of his attendants, he is also seeing love as having to do with the satisfaction of his desires (as he did earlier when he equated it with the public proclamation of love). This is to prefer the solicitous ship-board attendant, to cling to the yoghurt-hating identity, to want Scheherazade to go on telling her stories. It is to fail to see that the important thing is not to gratify desire, but to have the right desire and to perfect it. Simply to have this is to have it responded to. Pain is to school him to it. The journey is the more agonizing on account of the kind of attention he has received as king – precisely the kind to lead him away from purity of desire. This is well characterised in the accusation made against the steward of one of the false sisters by Lear's bluntly honest servant, whom he banished in rage for the opposite sort of attention. 'Smiling rogues' like this steward, he says,

> smooth every passion
> That in the natures of their lords rebel,
> Bring oil to fire, snow to the colder moods.[21]

They add to the seeming importance of errant desires, after the manner of modern advertising.

In the storm, Lear begins to learn the lessons of poverty. He feels compassion for his companion, the Fool, who is cold. He realizes, under the assault of the elements, that he has taken too little trouble about the homeless. As his mind begins to turn, the sight of someone who appears to be an unclothed beggar provokes him to this:

> Thou wert better in a grave than to answer with thy uncover'd body this extremity of the skies. Is man no more than this? Consider him well. Thou ow'st the worm no silk, the beast no hide, the sheep no wool, the cat no perfume. Ha? here's three on's are sophisticated. Thou art the thing itself: unaccommodated man is no more but such a poor, bare, fork'd animal as thou art. Off, off, you lendings! Come, unbutton here.
>
> [tearing off his clothes][22]

Although on the social level this behaviour is mad, in terms of his spiritual journey it makes sense. He is rejecting the outward for the inward. The apparent beggar – whom he later calls 'this philosopher'[23] – is man as he really is before God. This sight becomes an insight into himself. He calls himself and his companions 'sophisticated', that is, adulterated. Silk, hide, wool and perfume he sees as being plundered from creation to give man spurious importance. This is associated with court life, with its flattery and insincerity. It is a resting in the created rather than the uncreated – seeking meaning in what cannot give it. To say this does not mean that only nudists are sincere, God-trusting people, but that Lear intuitively recognizes that his love has been disproportionately placed on mere trappings. He has clung to the outward, to show – symbolically, to his false daughters rather than to his silent, true daughter. He is awakening to the blessedness of the poor in spirit to whom the kingdom of heaven belongs. He no longer wants to depend on 'all the large effects that troop with majesty',[24] but to be who he is, 'unaccommodated'

– without additions. This poverty of spirit is the beginning of his blessedness.

As he continues on his purgatorial journey he comes to a change of heart about his treatment of his true daughter

> that burning shame
> Detains him from Cordelia.[25]

His sense of unworthiness to be in her presence could be seen as a turning from the outward, to which he was too much attached when he demanded public declarations of love, to the inward and silent which he rejected when he disowned her for failing to respond to this demand. It is a conversion to true love. With it comes a rejection of the flattery that encouraged him to mistake his every thought for wisdom:

> they flatter'd me like a dog, and told me I had the white hairs in my beard ere the black ones were there. To say 'ay' and 'no' to everything that I said! 'Ay,' and 'no' too, was no good divinity.[26]

This is a rejection, as it were, of the shipboard companion who attends to his every wish. The 'divinity' or theology that whatever goes through man's head is the measure of the truth is replaced by a more realistic, because more humble, theology, taught him by the resistance of the rain, the wind and the thunder to his wishes. As contradiction can engender affection, as the difficulties of climbing a mountain can open one to the presence of nature, so Lear's suffering has brought him the knowledge that he is not omniscient or omnipotent.

He has learnt that his own desires are not the measure of everything. After a restorative sleep, Lear wakes to Cordelia's company. Something of the life of God, true love, is in him. He has learnt to be objective, to take God as he comes. This attitude, of acceptance of God's will, is summed up in the advice given to another character in the play telling him that he cannot choose the time of his death:

> Men must endure
> Their going hence even as their coming hither,
> Ripeness is all.[27]

'Ripeness is all' in this context refers to readiness for death, but the phrase describes well the openness to God's will that is at the heart of love for him. As he awakes Lear shows this in his humble self-knowledge. He knows that he has been undergoing purgatorial suffering, 'bound upon a wheel of fire'.[28] He awakens slowly to his physical presence:

> I will not swear these are my hands. Let's see,
> I feel this pin prick.[29]

He kneels in silent penitence to his true daughter, aware that he is old, foolish and has been unbalanced. He acknowledges her as his 'child Cordelia'.[30] This peaceful, humble objectivity is in moving contrast to his mad raving against his other daughters. It is shown again when Lear and Cordelia are taken to prison. He calmly accepts his lot and declares himself ready to be humble before her whom he treated so proudly:

> Come let's away to prison:
> We two alone will sing like birds i' th' cage;
> When thou dost ask me for blessing, I'll kneel down
> And ask of thee forgiveness.[31]

In terms of the life of God within him, this is a huge growth since his first abandonment of power. He seems now to see everything from an eternal vantage point where all is harmony:

> So we'll live,
> And pray, and sing, and tell old tales, and laugh
> And take upon's the mystery of things
> As if we were God's spies; and we'll wear out,
> In a wall'd prison packs and sects of great ones,
> That ebb and flow by th' moon.[32]

His emptying has allowed him to be filled with divine life: serenity and detachment from the factional desires of the 'packs and sects of great ones'. But there is further emptying to come, the ultimate deprivation, the death of Cordelia. The silence now is absolute: the silent love of God himself. As he dies, however, he becomes aware of her life in eternity:

Do you see this? Look on her! Look her lips,
Look there, look there![33]

To some critics of the play these words are just the final
pathetic illusion, all happiness crushed by her death. They
may be willing to accept that he grows spiritually, but see this
growth as being mocked by the cruel separation. On the
evidence of the play alone we cannot be absolutely certain
that the final pain is a final spiritual growth. Only faith can see
that in it. But we do have the evidence of what a real young
woman found, through faith, in a most painful separation
from her father. It is an intimation of celestial possibility.

CHAPTER ELEVEN

FATHER AND DAUGHTER

*An example of joyful spiritual
growth in suffering*

In our consideration of joy in tribulation we have so far
looked at the question (with the help of the imaginative
understanding given to us by literature) from the point of
view of theological understanding, in respect of conversion
and the virtues of faith, hope and charity. We have dwelt
mostly on how it can be reached. Here we shall dwell more
on the fact that it has been realized, using St Thérèse as our
example, to show that paradise in the midst of the suffering of
earth is more than a theoretical possibility. In Chapter Two we
saw how St Thérèse reacted to the irritation of the noise one
of her sisters made by trying to suffer 'with joy and peace' at
least in the intimacy of her soul and 'listening to it well'. The
latter phrase is a way of saying that she took it as it came, not
opposing herself to it. She was willing to be pleased with it if
it was, so to speak, the grey coat that God was pleased to see
her in. In the same way the laundry where she is splashed by
another of the sisters becomes for her 'this happy place where
I had received so many treasures'. There may be a note of
humorous irony in this description, but it is surely intended
to convey the spiritual truth that the ultimate good is to grow
in a generous love of God and that the opportunity to show
patience in this situation was for her a means of such growth.
These two little occasions give a microcosm of how
St Thérèse learnt to suffer well, to find joy and peace at the
heart of her suffering. In Chapter One it was claimed that the
point where tribulation is sweet and savoured for Christ is a
real human possibility. In St Thérèse we have that realization.

Obviously, to be convincing the example will have to show
more than patience with other people's little foibles. In fact,
her life was singularly marked by suffering of an incompara-
bly greater order and it was nonetheless joyful. There is a sort
of summary of this in her words to one of her sisters during
her final illness:

I have found happiness and joy on earth, but only in suffering, for I have suffered a lot here below. You must make this known to souls.[1]

We shall examine just one thread from this tapestry woven with pain: the suffering with which she was afflicted at the heart of one of the most vital relationships of her life, that with her father.[2] This was prophesied, prepared and symbolized by a vision she had as a child:

I saw, in front of the laundry that was just opposite, a man dressed exactly like papa, having the same height and gait, only he was *much more bent* ... his *head* was covered by a sort of tablecloth of indeterminate colour so that I couldn't see his face. He was wearing a hat like those of Papa. I saw him go forward with a regular pace, skirting my little garden ... Immediately a feeling of supernatural fear invaded my soul, but in a moment I reflected that Papa had no doubt returned and was hiding so as to surprise me; then I called very loudly with a voice trembling with emotion: 'Papa, Papa! ...' But the mysterious person seeming not to hear me, continued his regular step without even turning round; following him with my eyes, I saw him make his way towards the grove that cuts the big avenue in two, I was expecting to see him reappear on the other side of the great trees, but the prophetic vision had vanished ... All this only lasted a moment, but engraved itself so profoundly on my heart that today, after 15 years ... the memory of it is as present to me as if the vision were still before my eyes ...[3]

She later linked this experience with her father's mental breakdown, as a result of which he would sometimes muffle up his face. To her this was an echo of the passion of Jesus, as it was prophesied in the passage from Isaiah quoted in Chapter Nine. She added to her religious name 'of the Holy Face': meditation on the face of the suffering Christ was profoundly important to her. Some idea of the acuteness of the suffering that her father's breakdown caused her is given by this statement of what he meant to her:

> I cannot say how much I loved Papa, everything in him caused admiration in me; when he explained his thoughts to me (as if I had been a big girl) I said naïvely to him that of course, if he said all this to the great men of the government, they would take him to make him *King* and then France would be happy as it had never been . . .[4]

It would not be an exaggeration to say that the idea of God as an all-loving father that she formed as a child drew its inspiration from her own father, who was his image. It was therefore a great sacrifice for her to leave him to enter the convent, the more so as it was also a great sacrifice for him. The lives of both of them had been profoundly centred in the family. When his illness came and voices attributed it to her leaving him, the emotional pain must have been intense. Here is her account of the day her father left home for a mental institution, thirty-three days after she had been clothed as a nun:

> I remember that in the month of June 1888, at the moment of our first troubles, I said, 'I am suffering a lot, but I feel I could bear greater trials'. I wasn't thinking then of those that were reserved for me . . . I didn't know that on the 12th February, one month after my taking the habit, our dear father would drink the *most bitter*, and the most *humiliating* of all cups . . .
>
> Ah! that day I didn't say I was able to suffer any more!!! . . . words cannot express our anguish, so I am not going to try to describe it. One day, in Heaven, we shall love to speak to each other of our *glorious* trials, already are we not happy to have suffered them? . . . Yes the three years of Papa's martyrdom seem to me the most lovable, the most fruitful of all our life, I wouldn't give them for all the ecstasies and revelations of the saints, my heart overflows with gratitude thinking of this inestimable

> *treasure* that must cause a holy jealousy to the Angels of
> the Celestial court . . .[5]

What distinguishes the way St Thérèse sees her sufferings
here is the viewpoint. She sees them as they will appear in
heaven. From this point of view they will be so many ways in
which the soul was matured, enabled to receive the divine
life. Therefore she is already happy to have undergone them,
and the years which gave them to her seem the most lovable
and fruitful. She is finding paradise on earth because she is
looking at earthly tribulations as though she were in paradise.
Her heart is not in that which passes, but in the eternity that is
being prepared for her and therefore she is already, in the
midst of her trials, rejoicing in it and giving thanks for it.
There is a sense in which, in her inmost being, she is already
in paradise by virtue of her faith, hope and love. Only the
outward, time-bound part of her being is afflicted with
suffering. Whether a person enjoys paradise on earth comes
down to where they live: in the outer world of time and the
ego or in God – in the former case the pain of life gets into
their inner being, in the latter it only creates new spaces for
celebration.

More light on how St Thérèse accepts her suffering is given
in her correspondence with her sister and soul-mate Céline.
Later in the same month that their father was committed to a
mental institution she wrote:

> far from complaining to Jesus about the cross he is
> sending us, I cannot understand the *infinite* love that has
> led him to treat us in this way . . .[6]

The way in which she takes what is happening is informed by
a great awareness of the love that is behind the workings of
providence. To have this happen to their father was not only a
great grief, but also a great humiliation – the more so as it was
seen as being linked to her entry into the convent. She
understands this humiliation in the context of God's great and
loving purpose (which was achieved) of her sanctity:

What happiness to be humiliated, it's the only road to the making of saints ... Life is only a *dream*, soon, we shall wake up, and what joy ... the more our sufferings are great, the more our glory will be infinite ... Oh let us not lose the trial that Jesus sends us, it's a gold-mine to exploit, are we going to miss the opportunity?[7]

In one way or another, life gives everyone the opportunity it gave St Thérèse: it all depends how you take it. An analogy that suggests how her attitude leads to beatitude would be a person who always takes what other people say to him well, never taking offence – they would be likely to get on with other people happily, in contrast to the person who tended to take offence at what was said to them. St Thérèse takes what the Creator and Sustainer of the universe says to her, as it were, *very* well and consequently gets on with him, to put it mildly, happily. It is not to be supposed that she had at her disposal resources that the rest of us lack: later in the same letter she talks of setting about the work 'without *joy* without *courage* without strength'.[8] This absence of personal resource is even seen as making the undertaking (of profiting from suffering) easier, since it throws the weight of it, not on anything that she can claim as her own, but simply on God-given love.

The attitude that St Thérèse took to the troubles that afflicted the family found an echo from her sister Céline, who wrote back:

Oh! if only you knew how I see the good God in all our trials! Yes, everything is marked visibly with his divine finger.[9]

They lived in an atmosphere of faith that marked the whole of their family life. Its sustaining and transforming power did not come through a single individual but through their life together. Paradise in its terrestrial manifestation is characterized for them not just by their life of faith but by their sharing of their vision. St Thérèse speaks for both of them when she writes:

What a privilege Jesus gives us in sending us such a great *sorrow*, ah! ETERNITY will not be too long to thank him. He heaps his favours upon us as he heaped them upon the greatest saints . . .[10]

The reason why these troubles were seen as favours emerges in a later letter:

What then has Jesus done to detach our souls in this way from everything that is created? Ah, he has struck with a great blow . . . but it is a blow of love, God is wonderful, but above all he is lovable, let us love him then . . .[11]

In the same letter is a clear indication of her perspective:

Oh! what it costs to live, to stay on this earth of bitterness and anguish . . . But tomorrow . . . in one hour, we will be in port, what happiness! Ah how good it will be to contemplate Jesus *face to face* during *all* of eternity! Always always more love always more ecstatic joys . . . a cloudless happiness . . .[12]

This shows that the pain of exile was real, but that she saw time in its relative briefness and plunged her heart with faith and hope into the anticipation of the perfect love of eternity. Her heart was where her real treasure was, in paradise. This fact brought paradise to earth, as is witnessed by her capacity, even in the agony of her last illness, to enliven, amuse, inspire and, above all, love her sisters.

The layered nature of her experience – pain and anguish outwardly, as it were, but, in Milton's words, 'a paradise within'[13] – is brought out in her account of the day of her religious profession. She describes the day 'of my taking of the *veil*' as 'entirely *veiled* with tears'.[14] Her father was unable to be there because of his illness; others too were prevented from coming:

all was sadness and bitterness . . . However *peace*, always *peace* was found at the bottom of the chalice.[15]

Peace and pain coexist and peace is king. 'The chalice' is an allusion to the prayer of Jesus in the garden of Gethsemane, 'Father, if thou art willing, remove this cup from me; nevertheless not my will, but thine, be done'.[16] A comment that St Thérèse made during her final illness on this episode in the life of Jesus illuminates the way she found peace at the bottom of the chalice:

> Our Lord in the Garden of Olives enjoyed all the delights of the Trinity, and nevertheless his agony was not the less cruel on account of it. It is a mystery, but I assure you that I understand something of it through what I experience myself.[17]

It is clear that her peace is no anodyne; it does not blot out pain. Yet it is heavenly. 'It is a mystery', as we should expect paradise on earth to be since it is the presence here of something that eye has not seen nor ear heard. The limits of our perception veil it, veil it with tears.

A letter written by St Thérèse to her sister Céline on the eve of the tearful day offers further reflections on this shrouded dialectic of heaven and earth. She sees what is happening with the intuition of faith:

> Oh! Céline, how can I tell you what is happening in my soul? . . . It is torn, but I sense that this wound is made by a friendly hand, by a hand *divinely jealous!* . . .
> . . . it is Jesus alone who has directed this affair, it's him, and I have recognized his touch of *love* . . .[18]

She sees it, remembering the face of Jesus crucified, with the vision of hope:

Céline! . . . the shadows are waning and the form of this world is passing away, soon, yes soon we shall see the unknown and loved face which ravishes us by its tears.[19]

She sees it with the generosity of love:

> Céline, let us accept with a good heart the thorn that Jesus offers us, tomorrow's feast will be a feast of tears for us, but I sense that Jesus will be so consoled! . . .[20]

And she yearns to communicate the peace she has:

> I am charged with writing to you to console you but I
> have no doubt acquitted myself badly . . . Ah! . . . if I could
> communicate to you the peace that Jesus has put in my
> soul in the thick of my tears . . .[21]

The grief occasioned by her father's illness is an example of
the suffering St Thérèse endured. The explicitness of her
commentary on it gives some idea of how she savoured
suffering for Christ. We also have, in a letter to a missionary
priest that she adopted as a spiritual brother, her exposition
of our text from *The Imitation of Christ*, a book which meant
a lot to her:

> St John of the Cross said, 'The smallest movement of pure
> love is more profitable to the Church than all works put
> together'. If that is so, how profitable must your troubles
> and trials be to the Church, since it is for love of Jesus
> alone that you suffer them *with joy*. Truly, my brother, I
> cannot find fault with you, since in you are realized these
> words of *The Imitation*: 'When you find suffering sweet
> and you love it for love of Jesus Christ, you will have
> found Paradise on earth'. This Paradise is indeed that of
> the missionary and carmelite; the joy that worldly people
> seek in the bosom of pleasures is only a fugitive shadow,
> but our joy, sought and tasted in works and sufferings, is
> a truly sweet reality and a foretaste of the happiness of
> Heaven.[22]

She goes on to tell the story of a sweet and innocent looking
lobster that escaped from a cooking-pot and struggled diabo-
lically with the sister attempting to recapture it and comments
parenthetically 'one mustn't believe the compliments of
creatures',[23] a comment which places, with great lightness of
touch, her attitude to merely worldly joys. Her confidence was
placed in celestial joy.

The degree of that confidence, and what that joy consisted
in, is indicated by the testimony given by one of her sisters in
the investigations that preceded her canonization:

In carmel, I knew her completely celestial, earth was no longer anything for her. She said to me, in a thousand different ways, that what she envisaged above all in the thought of heaven, wasn't the personal enjoyment that she would experience in this abode, but the fact that she would love God more there; that she would be loved by God and that she would find there the means to make God loved more.

Confidence in God had become as it were the special seal of her soul. She had been attracted to it since her most tender childhood, and I had done all I could to develop this disposition. She said to me one day that she had been struck since her childhood by this verse of Job: 'Even if he killed me, I would hope in him'.[24]

She learnt this confidence of course from Christ whose hope in his Father persevered in death, even death on a cross. This confidence changed the world, bringing heaven to it. A world so transformed is experienced very differently.

CHAPTER TWELVE

THREE DAYS AND PARADISE ON EARTH

*Jesus Christ is the source, the inspiration
and the joy of paradise on earth*

The title of à Kempis' book, *The Imitation of Christ*, indicates that what he has to say about finding joy in suffering is learnt from Jesus Christ. He is also the teacher of the saints whose lives and words endorse what à Kempis says. References and allusions to his teaching in the gospels have guided our discussion. The literature that has illustrated it, whatever the affiliations of the authors, has been written in the context of a Christian culture. It is therefore appropriate to draw together the threads of our discussion by turning our attention more directly upon him. As Hopkins says:

> Hither then, last or first,
> To hero of Calvary, Christ's feet –
> Never ask if meaning it, wanting it, warned of it – men go.[1]

St Irenaeus, in describing Christ as the summing-up of mankind, alludes to St Paul's description of God's purpose 'which he set forth in Christ as a plan for the fullness of time, to unite all things in him, things in heaven and things on earth'.[2] Christ sums up mankind; he is the perfect realization of humanity; he is God-with-us; he is heaven come down to earth. The life that St Thérèse led, finding paradise on earth, was an imitation of him. In his life is the epitome and source of the attitude that this book has attempted to describe: one perfectly turned to God, formed and informed by faith, hope and love. It is a life entirely free of self, completely filled with space for God, the life of one

> who, though he was in the form of God, did not count equality a thing to be grasped, but emptied himself, taking the form of a servant, being born in the likeness of men. And being found in human form he humbled

himself and became obedient unto death, even death on a cross. Therefore God has highly exalted him and bestowed on him the name which is above every name, that at the name of Jesus every knee should bow, in heaven and on earth and under the earth, and every tongue confess that Jesus Christ is Lord, to the glory of God the Father.[3]

This chapter focuses on this source and its implications for finding paradise on earth. Any such focus runs a two-fold risk: that of merely echoing what has become the conventional thing to say about it and that of missing the reality through being blinded by the excess of light. It is hoped that such a risk is forestalled by what has come before: that the investigation of the attitude that Christ taught from the point of view of ordinary experience and literature will help it to be seen in its human reality rather than as a polished display, and that the refraction of the light of Christ through the life of St Thérèse will already have intimated its reality. By way of relating what is said here to what has come before, reference will be made to the poem by W.B. Yeats which gives Chapter Three its title. The reader may find it helpful to have another look at it.

In its terrestrial aspect, the cross was an experience of complete desolation – utterly comfortless, painful and humiliating. Nothing earthly was available to offer support and therefore the dependence on God had to be absolute. Faith in his loving providence had to be perfect to see what was happening as an expression of his love despite the suffering involved. Hope had to be at its utmost – the hope of being 'today . . . in Paradise'[4] – to avoid despair in this desolation. Love had to be at its most generous to accept what was going on without bitterness. This love involved an emptiness of personal will: Jesus prayed in the garden of Gethsemane, 'Not my will, but thine, be done'.[5] The emptiness of the cross was an absolute absence of any ego-life in the negative sense indicated by Yeats' description of gazing 'in the bitter glass': its 'fatal image' is killed on the cross by absolute reliance on divine (eternal) life (which we can use the theological virtues to analyze) in an experience of such desolation that there was nothing for any ego-life to be invested in. This is not of course to say that Jesus lived in any way egoistically or other than with a perfectly divine life before he was crucified: he slew the 'fatal image' *for us*. At a level that is deeper than any ego-life humanity is one, and here, if we are willing to open ourselves to it, the victory has been won. The cross is 'the holy tree' where

> the holy branches start,
> And all the trembling flowers they bear.
> The changing colours of its fruit
> Have dowered the stars with merry light;
> The surety of its hidden root
> Has planted quiet in the night;
> The shaking of its leafy head
> Has given the waves their melody . . .[6]

In our communion with Jesus not only do we have access to this (eternal) life, but we have the opportunity to participate through our sufferings in slaying the 'fatal image' (echo of the discordant and dividing assertion of the ego) displayed by 'the glass of outer weariness'. When our sufferings, joined to his, enable, not just for ourselves but for others as well, the dowering of the stars with this merry light (the consequence of the 'fatal image' dying), then we are savouring them for Christ and these stars illuminate the earth with the radiance of paradise. We become emptied of egoism and filled with the divine life, a life that illuminates others as well as ourselves, awakes them to the indwelling of the divine in them.

The divine underwriting of the forsaking of egoism is indicated in the teaching of Jesus: in the wedding guest who is asked to move to a higher place; in the last who will be first; in the meek who shall inherit the earth. It is echoed in the Magnificat with its exaltation of the humble. It is demonstrated in the resurrection, pledge and earnest of Heaven. The fact that Jesus rose from the dead shows that suffering need not be loss: it can be the forsaking of a limited life to receive an unlimited life. The walking, talking and eating with his disciples of the resurrected Jesus is paradise on earth; in sharing his attitude to suffering – suffering with a heart turned to God with faith, hope and love – we are sharing that paradise. The suffering belongs only to time; the paradisal element to eternity – it is both present and enduring. The form of this present world is passing away; the joyful life of the next is being born. On the cross the disfigured Jesus seems to lose his identity; in fact he is receiving the name which is above every name; humbled, he is exalted. Those who suffer may feel that they are being torn apart, that they no longer are anyone, but, sharing his spirit and his attitude, they are being given, as promised in the Book of Revelation, a new identity:

> a white stone, with a new name written on the stone which no one knows except him who receives it.[7]

This whole process of realizing (in both senses of the word) the eternal life present in time, joy in suffering, paradise on earth, takes place in the eucharist. It is celebrated in union with the angels and the saints, inhabitants of Heaven. It takes the troubles of time, unites them with the sufferings of Christ and gives the life of the resurrection. It is a thanksgiving: these troubles, as well as every joy, are offered up in that spirit which sees God's loving purpose behind all that happens and *is grateful for it*. It is the coming of Heaven – of the divine life of Jesus – to earth. Everything is offered to God and everything is received from him. This communion with him is unity with others, in whom he dwells, at the deepest level, and so a beginning of Heaven. The eucharist is the focal point of the way of life that leads to paradise on earth: that of accepting faithfully, hopefully and lovingly everything that comes from the hand of God.

In it earth is lifted up to Heaven. This is symbolized by the towering of the church into the sky, by the sanctuary being on a higher level, by the raised-up altar and by the lifting up of the bread and wine. The symbolism of the eucharist, link between heaven and earth, echoes and focuses the symbolism of nature. The sky is the natural sign of heaven towards which the architecture and ritual of the Church point. A striking instance of its being experienced as such is given by Céline, sister of St Thérèse, in her relation of her experience immediately following the saint's death. Her grief seemed to be echoed by the overcast sky as she walked outside. If only, she thought with her head bowed, there were some sign, if at least it wasn't such an overcast sky. She looked up and the sky was entirely clear, stars shining in it. To St Thérèse herself, all of nature spoke of God's great love. She found paradise on earth, seeing everything in the light of Heaven. She was once moved to tears by the sight of a mother hen with her wing over her chicks because it brought to her mind God's great loving care for her; in her last illness she saw through the window the setting sun shining golden on the trees and commented that her radiance came entirely from God in the same way that the brightness of the trees came from the sun.[8]

To one who has reached the point of which à Kempis speaks, all of creation, all of experience speaks of the transcendent. The ordinary becomes the heavenly, trans-formed in the way Hopkins describes in *The Windhover*:

> No wonder of it: sheer plod makes plough down sillion
> Shine, and blue-bleak embers, ah my dear,
> Fall, gall themselves, and gash gold-vermilion.[9]

The 'dearest freshness deep down things'[10] is everywhere known, because the Creator and his unfailing promise are known. It is a promise that can never be betrayed, as the American poet Hart Crane obscurely realised in these lines, which he felt achieved 'a kind of revelation':[11]

> The imaged Word, it is, that holds
> Hushed willows anchored in its glow.
> It is the unbetrayable reply
> Whose accent no farewell can know.[12]

The Word, through whom all things were made, is imaged in the creation. One who knows him knows the meaning, the love and the joy in it: 'willows', symbol of the sorrows of this our exile, are held hushed – there is, in such a person's deepest heart, no sound of lamentation, only the glow of his love. There is never, in all eternity, any parting from this love. It is paradise on earth.

NOTES

Chapter One: The Challenge

1. Book Two, chapter 12, my translation.
2. Meister Eckhart, *Sermons & Treatises*, Volume III, Translated and Edited by M.O'C. Walshe (Shaftesbury, 1987), p. 93.
3. Ludovicus Blosius, *A Book of Spiritual Instruction*, translated by Bertrand A. Wilberforce O.P. (London, 1925), p. 84.
4. Sainte Thérèse de L'Enfant-Jésus et de la Sainte-Face, *J'entre Dans La Vie: Derniers Entretiens* (Paris, 1983), p. 37. This and subsequent citations from St Thérèse are given in my own translation from the French.
5. John Climacus, *The Ladder of Divine Ascent*, translated by Colm Luibheid and Norman Russell (London, 1982), p. 231.
6. Book Two, chapter 6.
7. *J'entre Dans La Vie: Derniers Entretiens*, p. 178.
8. T.S. Eliot, *Four Quartets*, in *Collected Poems 1909–1962* (London, 1970), p. 189.
9. Act IV, scene iii, lines 23–4. This and subsequent quotations from Shakespeare are from *The Riverside Shakespeare* (Boston, 1974).

Chapter Two: Tribulation

1. *The Poems of Gerard Manley Hopkins*, Edited by W.H. Gardner and N.H. MacKenzie (Oxford, 1970), p. 260.
2. *Ibid.* p. 59
3. Act 1, scene ii, lines 418–19.
4. *The Poems of Gerard Manley Hopkins*, p. 61.
5. *The Loss of the Eurydice, ibid.* p. 74.
6. Sainte Thérèse de l'Enfant-Jésus, *Manuscrits Autobiographiques* (Lisieux, 1957), pages 300–301.
7. Samuel Beckett, *Molloy, Malone Dies, The Unnamable* (London, 1976), p. 243.
8. *Macbeth*, act II, scene iii, line 50.
9. St Luke, chapter 12, verses 13–21.

Chapter Three: The Two Trees

1. William Blake, *The Clod & the Pebble*, page 505 in *The Norton Anthology of Poetry* (New York, London, 1970).
2. See *La Grande Dame du Pur Amour: Sainte Catherine de Gênes – Vie et Doctrine et Traité du Purgatoire* (Paris, 1960), translated by Pierre Debongnie (Paris, 1960), p. 99.
3. *Manuscrits Autobiographiques*, p. 183.
4. *Ibid.* p. 160.
5. Book XII, lines 585–7.
6. St Matthew, chapter 5, verse 45.
7. Act 1, scene i, line 51.
8. *The Poems of William Blake*, edited by W.H. Stevenson and David V. Erdman (London, 1977), p. 162.
9. St Matthew, chapter 5, verse 3.
10. Chapter 30, verse 19.

11. *The Collected Poems of W.B. Yeats* (London, 1939), pages 54–55.
12. See *The Poems of William Blake*, edited by W.H. Stevenson and David V. Erdman (London, 1977), p. 635: 'it is an empty imitation of a man, not his real self – and so tragedy follows when a person depends on the shadow instead of the reality'.

Chapter Four: Killing Scheherazade
  1. St Matthew, chapter 13, verses 45–46.
  2. St John, chapter 10, verse 10.
  3. Samuel Beckett, *Proust and Three Dialogues* (London, 1976), pages 13–14.
  4. *Waiting for Godot* (London, 1971), p. 89
  5. Samuel Beckett, *Krapp's Last Tape and Embers* (London, 1973); p. 13, *Footfalls* (London, 1976).
  6. Samuel Beckett, *Molloy, Malone Dies, The Unnamable* (London, 1976), p. 89.
  7. *Ibid.* p. 418.
  8. St Luke, chapter 17, verse 33.
  9. Chapter 2, verse 17.
 10. *Adonais*, stanza 52, line 4; p. 636 of *The Norton Anthology of Poetry* (New York, London, 1970).
 11. Samuel Beckett, *Ill Seen, Ill Said* (London, 1982), p. 59.
 12. St Luke, chapter 14, verse 26.
 13. St Mark, chapter 8, verse 36.
 14. *The English Poems of George Herbert*, edited by C.A. Patrides (London, 1981), pages 166–167.
 15. *Confessions*, Book 1, chapter 1.
 16. Colossians, chapter 3, verse 3.
 17. The first Letter of St John, chapter 5, verse 4.

Chapter Five: Ultimate Reinsurance
  1. St Luke, chapter 14, verses 12–14.
  2. The First Letter of St John, chapter 4, verse 16.
  3. St Luke chapter 9, verse 58.
  4. St John, chapter 4, verse 34.
  5. *The Poems of Gerard Manley Hopkins*, edited by W.H. Gardner and N.H. MacKenzie (Oxford, 1970), p. 85.
  6. *The English Poems of George Herbert*, edited by C.A. Patrides (London, 1981), pages 70–71.
  7. The letter of St James, chapter 1, verses 2–3.
  8. *The Marriage of Heaven and Hell, III: Proverbs of Hell* (line 57), p. 110 in *The Poems of William Blake*, edited by W.H. Stevenson and David V. Erdman (London, 1977).
  9. St Luke, chapter 12, verse 7.

Chapter Six: Trusting
  1. *Hamlet*, Act III, scene i, line 57.
  2. Romans, chapter 8, verse 28.
  3. Genesis, chapter 12, verse 1.
  4. *J'entre Dans La Vie: Derniers Entretiens* (Paris, 1983), p. 58.
  5. St Matthew, chapter 10, verse 16.
  6. *Confessions*, Book VI, chapter 6.

7. St Matthew, chapter 13, verses 45–46.
8. Job, chapter 1, verse 21.
9. cf St Matthew, chapter 6, verse 33.
10. St John, chapter 5, verse 41.
11. In her act of offering of herself as a holocaust victim to the merciful love of God, *Manuscrits Autobiographiques*, p. 319.

Chapter Seven: The Locked-Away Mind
1. St Matthew, chapter 6, verse 34.
2. Act IV, scene 4, lines 36–39.
3. Chapter 8.
4. *Ibid.*
5. *Ibid.*
6. *Break, Break, Break*, line 15. Page 704 in *The Norton Anthology of Poetry* (New York, London, 1970).
7. Chapter 8.
8. Chapter 2, verse 13.
9. *Quaestionum Evangeliorum*, Book 2, Quaestio XXXIII, paragraph 2.
10. *Ode on Intimations of Immortality from Recollections of Early Childhood*, lines 63–6, page 553 in *The Norton Anthology of Poetry* (New York, London, 1970).

Chapter Eight: Remembering Zion
1. *Little Gidding*, section III, page 219 in *Collected Poems 1909–1962* (London, 1970).
2. Chapter 15, verse 13.
3. See Chapter Three.
4. Psalm 136, Grail translation.
5. *The Republic*, Book 7.
6. St Matthew, chapter 13, verses 45–6.
7. St Matthew, chapter 6, verse 33.
8. Chapter 64, verse 6, Authorised Version.
9. In her act of offering of herself as a holocaust victim to the merciful love of God, *Manuscrits Autobiographiques*. p. 319.

Chapter Nine: Love and the Grey Coat
1. Act IV, scene iv, lines 135–146.
2. *J'entre Dans La Vie: Derniers Entretiens* (Paris, 1983), p. 35.
3. *Ibid.*
4. See *The Hour of Jesus, The Passion and the Resurrection of Jesus according to John: Test and Spirit* by Ignace de la Potterie S.J., translated Dom Gregory Murray O.S.B., St Paul Publications (Slough, 1989).
5. Act III, scene i, lines 2–7.
6. *The Elixir* in *The English Poems of George Herbert* edited by C.A. Patrides (London, 1981), page 188.
7. See St Luke, chapter 10, verses 38–42.
8. 1 Corinthians, chapter 13, verses 4–7.
9. *The Brothers Karamazov*, translated Garnett (London, 1939), Book Two, chapter 4.
10. St Matthew, chapter 5, verses 44–45.
11. St Matthew, chapter 25, verse 40.

12. W.R. Inge, *Light, Life and Love: Selections From the German Mystics of the Middle Ages* (London, 1904), p. 7.
13. Chapter 53, verses 2–3.
14. Act V, scene ii, lines 295–6.
15. *God's Grandeur*, p. 66 of *The Poems of Gerard Manley Hopkins*, edited by W.H. Gardner and N.H. MacKenzie (Oxford, 1970).
16. St Luke, chapter 12, verse 34.
17. *J'entre Dans La Vie: Derniers Entretiens* (Paris, 1983), p. 37.
18. The Letter to the Hebrews, chapter 12, verse 6; The Letter of St James, chapter 1, verse 2; The First Letter of St Peter, chapter 1, verse 6.
19. Psalm 125, Grail translation.

Chapter Ten: Ripeness Is All

1. *Jerusalem*, introduction to Chapter 3, p. 735 in *The Poems of William Blake*, edited by W.H. Stevenson and David V. Erdman (London, 1977). The stanza quoted is the last in a poem beginning 'I saw a monk of Charlemagne'.
2. Cf. St Luke, chapter 17, verse 21.
3. *King Lear* Act V, scene ii, lines 9–11.
4. Job, chapter 1, verse 21.
5. Romans, chapter 8, verse 18.
6. Lines 16–20, p. 892 in *The Norton Anthology of Poetry*.
7. *Eternity*, quoted in Chapter Three.
8. *King Lear* Act 1, scene i, line 62.
9. Act 1, scene i, line 87.
10. Act 1, scene i, line 193.
11. Act 1, scene i, line 197.
12. Act 1, scene i, lines 238–40.
13. Act 1, scene i, line 250.
14. St Matthew, chapter 5, verse 3.
15. *King Lear* Act 1, scene iv, lines 230–1.
16. Act 1, scene iv, line 306.
17. Act 1, scene v, line 24.
18. Act II, scene iv, lines 258–60.
19. Act II, scene iv, line 261.
20. Act II, scene iv, line 263.
21. Act II scene ii, line 73, lines 75–7.
22. Act III, scene iv, lines 101–109.
23. Act III, scene iv, line 154.
24. Act I, scene i, lines 131–2.
25. Act IV, scene iii, lines 46–7.
26. Act IV, scene vi, lines 96–100.
27. Act V, scene ii, lines 9–11.
28. Act IV, scene vii, lines 45–6.
29. Act IV, scene vii, lines 54–5.
30. Act IV, scene vii, line 69.
31. Act V, scene iii, lines 8–11.
32. Act V, scene iii, lines 11–13, 16–19.
33. Act V, scene iii, lines 311–12.

Chapter Eleven: Father and Daughter

1. *J'entre Dans La Vie: Derniers Entretiens*, page 104.
2. She also suffered acute physical pain. This is excellently documented in Guy Gaucher's *La Passion de Thérèse de Lisieux* (Paris, 1973).
3. *Manuscrits Autobiographiques*, pages 48–9.
4. *Ibid.* p. 51.
5. *Ibid.* pages 182–3.
6. Letter of 28th February 1990, p. 459 of *Correspondance Générale*, volume 1 (Paris, 1972).
7. Ibid. pages 459–60.
8. *Ibid.* p. 460.
9. Letter of March 1st, 1889, *Correspondance Générale*, volume 1, p. 461.
10. Letter to Céline of March 5th 1889, p. 463 of *Correspondance Générale*, volume 1.
11. Letter to Céline of July 14th, 1889, p. 494 of *Correspondance Générale*, volume 1.
12. *Ibid.*
13. *Paradise Lost*, Book XII, line 587.
14. *Manuscrits autobiographiques*, p. 192.
15. *Ibid.*
16. St Luke, chapter 22, verse 42.
17. *J'entre Dans La Vie: Derniers Entretiens*, p. 58.
18. Letter of 23rd September, 1890, p. 584 of *Correspondance Générale*, volume 1.
19. *Ibid.* p. 586.
20. *Ibid.* p. 585.
21. *Ibid.* p. 585.
22. Letter of 19th March 1897 to Father Roulland, p. 961 of *Correspondance Générale*, volume 2.
23. *Ibid.* p. 962.
24. *Procès de Béatification et Canonisation de Sainte Thérèse de L'Enfant-Jésus et de la Sainte-Face, 1: Procès Informatif Ordinaire* (Rome, 1973), p. 155.

Chapter Twelve: Three Days and Paradise on Earth

1. *The Wreck of the Deutschland*, stanza 8, on page 54 of *The Poems of Gerard Manley Hopkins,* edited by W.H. Gardner and N.H. MacKenzie (Oxford, 1970).
2. Ephesians, chapter 1, verse 9–10.
3. Philippians, chapter 2, verses 6–11.
4. St Luke, chapter 23, verse 43.
5. St Luke, chapter 22, verse 42.
6. *The Two Trees*, pages 54–5 of *The Collected Poems of W.B. Yeats* (London, 1939). See Chapter Three.
7. Chapter 2, verse 17.
8. *J'entre Dans La Vie: Derniers Entretiens*, p. 213.
9. *The Poems of Gerard Manley Hopkins,* edited by W.H. Gardner and N.H. MacKenzie (Oxford, 1970), p. 69.
10. *God's Grandeur, Ibid.* p. 66.
11. R.S. Lewis *The Poetry of Hart Crane: A Critical Study* (Princeton, 1967), p. 148. Crane's comment referred to an earlier draft.
12. Hart Crane, *Complete Poems*, Edited by Brom Weber (Newcastle upon Tyne, 1984), p. 59. The lines quoted are the last stanza of *Voyages*.